What to Do
with Sunday Morning

What to Do
with Sunday Morning

Harold M. Daniels

The Westminster Press
Philadelphia

First edition

Published by The Westminster Press ®
Philadelphia, Pennsylvania

PRINTED IN THE UNITED STATES OF AMERICA
9 8 7 6 5 4 3 2 1

Library of Congress Cataloging in Publication Data

Daniels, Harold M   1927–
  What to do with Sunday morning.

  Includes bibliographical references.
  1. Liturgics. 2. Public worship. I. Title.
BV176.D36   264   78–21040
ISBN 0–664–24237–5

To the "saints" of St. Andrew
among whom I learned the meaning
of Christian community

Contents

Preface

What can we do with Sunday morning?

One of the most urgent needs of church life continues to be liturgical renewal. The struggle for worship that is truly contemporary is as crucial as ever. This book was written to offer practical help for those faced with these urgencies, those responsible for planning and leading in worship Sunday after Sunday.

The central aim of worship is to give glory to God. But flowing from the worship of God is the healing of human life. True worship contributes to human growth and wholeness. In these pages, a worship is called for that recognizes both the God-centeredness of worship and the human growth that should be its result.

The liturgical gathering is seen as the central action of the church's life together. In worship the congregation expresses itself as a "body." Worship is the primary action that gives direction and meaning to all else that a congregation does in its own life and in the life of the larger community beyond the church walls. Great care therefore needs to be given to the church's liturgical life, for all else that the church does is either strengthened or weakened by the quality of its worship. To help congregations find a liturgical style that is life-giving, this book provides a theology to undergird lit-

urgy, guidelines to develop liturgy, and practical suggestions
for doing liturgy.

Worship has been a particular focus of both my pastoral
ministry and my academic studies. From those backgrounds
I have tried to select for discussion those emphases which
seem most practical for planning worship. I have written for
the benefit of those who have this responsibility.

I am deeply indebted to the St. Andrew United Presbyterian Church of Albuquerque, New Mexico, which I served
as pastor. This congregation has been the liturgical laboratory for the thinking and doing of liturgy throughout the
evolution of this book. But more than providing the setting
for the redevelopment of liturgy, this congregation knows
and experiences the meaning of liturgy. Worship is vital to
its life. At St. Andrew, worship is a communal experience—
a joyous celebration of the community of faith. The dedica-
tion and the creativity of the session's Committee on Worship
and the Arts have been an inspiration, making tangible the
highest hopes of a renewed liturgical life.

The help of Professor Howard Rice, of San Francisco
Theological Seminary, has been most valuable and encouraging.

The patience, tolerance, and sacrifice of my family during
the writing of this book and the many years of study that
preceded it, were indispensable to the completion of goals,
and are most gratefully and lovingly appreciated.

H.M.D.

Eastertide 1978

Chapter I

The Changing Liturgy

Eleven o'clock Sunday morning has come once more in Old Greystone and Ivy Church. The people are assembled. The organ prelude ends. Pastor Goodfellow drones: "Let us worship God. The Lord is in his holy temple; let all the earth keep silence before him."

The organist plays the introduction to the first hymn. At the last line of the introduction, the congregation stands together, cued by long-established custom. The people sing halfheartedly, "Holy, Holy, Holy! Lord God Almighty . . ." What follows is familiar, the result of constant repetition, Sunday after Sunday, year after year. Worship in the average Protestant church hasn't changed much across the years.

The sermon ended, the final hymn sung, Pastor Goodfellow pronounces the benediction. The choir sings in response, "Amen, Amen." The organist adds the final touch. Filing out the door, the worshipers feel obliged to say, "That was a good sermon, Reverend." The people return to other tasks and activities, which, they tend to feel, constitute *real life.*

Sunday after Sunday, that one hour is predictable, unimaginative, uninspiring. Nothing much ever happens in Sunday worship; few of us really expect much to happen. Most of us are at least moderately bored. Others of us conclude that the Sunday worship service is largely irrelevant to our lives and the issues important to us. It is out of touch with modern life.

Most of us still attend worship out of habit, knowing that God does work even in the dullest worship service. But some drop in only now and then, while others never come anymore.

1. THE IMPORTANCE OF WORSHIP

When we begin to recognize the importance of worship, we see that much of our worship is tragic. Worship is important because religious faith is important for the fullest development of human life, both personal and social.

Religion is life lived at the deepest level of meaning. To be religious is to live life on a deeper plane and within a broader context of values and meanings than those which immediately preoccupy us. When we seek life's values and meanings only within the confines of our immediate needs and situation, life tends to be empty, aimless, and meaningless.

Utilizing the richness of symbolic and mythological language and ritual, religion encounters the human questions in depth, affirms the worth of life and the trustworthiness of the ultimate context in which life is lived.

Religion recovers a sense of the "hanging-togetherness" of all existence in which the big meanings of *all* life and the smaller meanings of *my* life somehow flow together. My smaller, immediate, personal meanings need to be a part of the more inclusive meanings that encompass *all* human life and experience. This is what St. Augustine meant when he prayed, "Thou hast made us, O Lord, for Thyself and our heart shall find no rest till it rest in Thee." God is the ultimate context "in whom we live and move and have our being." To be *in* God is to live life's smaller meanings in the light of life's cosmic dimensions.

Worship is the primary human experience that conveys, shapes, and reinforces religious conviction. Worship is important, therefore, because it is the point in our lives where we celebrate everything that gives meaning to life. It expresses our ultimate concerns, nurtures our ideals, and focuses upon human life as it is meant to be. It is the occasion of our seeking unity with God and other human beings. Worship therefore has a humanizing role, creative of life.

Both personally and culturally, we lack a sense of purpose and direction, unless there is some point in common experience where we celebrate life's greatest values, where we anticipate the fulfillment of the vision of human possibility, where we commemorate those great events of the human story (past and future) which give life direction, where we find union with the depths of reality by opening ourselves to the enabling power of the presence of Love. Worship ought to be that moment in life in which we act out all that gives meaning, purpose, and direction to every dimension of human relationships, personal and social.

Worship therefore serves our most basic human need. Dutch Roman Catholic theologian Edward Schillebeeckx questions whether human life can possibly be meaningful without thanksgiving celebrations. He sees the church and its worship as "the poetry in the prose of our lives," its task "perhaps as mankind's representative, bearing witness to, expressing, proclaiming and commemorating in grateful celebration the inexpressible mystery from which this world may live." This is "the first humanizing task of the Church—to celebrate, to thank, and to commemorate, and in this way to engage in a relationship with reality."[1]

This humanizing role of liturgy adds a sense of urgency to our task of developing a liturgical style that is in tune with contemporary experience. Whenever worship fails to give life direction and meaning, its failure is grievous. Unless we recover a worship that gives depth to life, the Christian faith

may well be pushed to the periphery of life unable to give
vitality to personal, social, and cultural relationships.

2. CONTEMPORARY WORSHIP

Worship fulfills its creative role only when it is contemporary. Both religious doctrines and liturgical forms born in
past ages ultimately get out of touch with life unless they
undergo a cultural evolution. But when the forms of faith
evolve in a way appropriate to the cultural setting, they can
provide a vision of the highest hope of which that culture is
capable.

What we believe as Christians, and the way we worship,
therefore needs to be fluid and evolving, never static and
fixed. We need to express theology and liturgy in fresh forms,
appropriate to our place in history. This task calls for innovation, creativity, and risk. An openness to the world, to life
and to change, is needed if we are to be successful in developing a faith that is relevant to the modern age.

The issue is therefore much deeper than a concern for
style, the use of mod music, guitars, or colloquial language.
Worship may incorporate all of these and still be out of touch
with the significant issues of contemporary life. The more
important test is whether or not worship expresses contemporary, existential issues and relates persons to the living of
life today. An evolving liturgy will no doubt include modern
media and art forms, but the issue of relevancy to modern life
is the primary concern.

The pursuit of relevance, however, can be perilous if liturgy is cut off from the past or the future. The present is filled
with ramifications of the totality of time. We need to take
seriously not only the present but also the past and the future,
if liturgy is to nurture our lives adequately.

It is true that interest in the past can degenerate into either
nostalgia or antiquarianism. Nevertheless, we cannot afford

to discard the past even though we sometimes relate to it in ways that are not constructive. A proper appropriation of the past into present experience is vital to our self-identity as persons and as a society. The past lives within us as memory. In worship we recall the events of the origin and history of the faith, most particularly the Christ event. This communal memory enriches life and gives us insight into who we are. To know and celebrate the past is an important part of our journey into the future.

Just as it is important to allow the past to inform our self-understanding, so it is also important that we face into the future. The future sprouts within us as hope. Worship should nourish human hope, and give focus and definition to the content of that hope. Worship should be a celebration of the possibilities of the future, an expression of expectancy for the coming of God's kingdom.

Thus liturgy needs to encompass the expansiveness of time, the process and growth through past ages, and the hope of future evolution and becoming. Both memory and hope are aspects of a living faith that gives meaning and direction to our contemporary worship.

3. REDIRECTING THE FOCUS OF WORSHIP

Past worship practice has varied greatly in style. It is helpful to understand the principal directions of the worship styles we have inherited, so that we may recognize their values and shortcomings and be assisted in redirecting worship in ways appropriate to the contemporary task.

Worship styles have often been described as objective and subjective. The classification is an oversimplification, because each style has some elements of the other. But no other classification is as effective in pointing out the general differences in existing liturgical styles.

Objective worship may be described as worship that

moves Godward, "vertically," and stresses God's transcendence and mystery. The principal response of the worshiper is to adore God and to fulfill duty. The primary orientation is to the past, to what God has done. Worship is understood as being communal, sacramental, and ritualistic.

Subjective worship may be described as worship that moves personward, "horizontally," and stresses God's immanence. This worship centers on the self and on personal need; it stresses the faith of the worshiper. The principal intent of the worshiper is to seek God's blessing and be inspired. The primary orientation is to the present, to what God is doing. Worship is understood in a highly individualistic manner, and is emotional and spontaneous.

Objective liturgical worship rarely finds God in human affairs; subjective, evangelical worship rarely rises above individual feelings. Objective worship tends to retard people's growth by failing to give primacy to human life; subjective worship tends to hinder people's growth by keeping them in their infancy. Classical theology, upon which objective worship is based, is often antiquarian, out of touch with the contemporary world. The theology of pietism, upon which subjective worship is based, is often vaguely sentimental, divorced from historical roots.

We ought to avoid the extremes of both subjective and objective worship and seek to recover from both of these the aspects of worship which are appropriate to contemporary life.

Because life is important, liturgy needs to be subjective. But the subjectivity will be different from what we have inherited. Concern for the meaning and quality of life, for human growth and relationships, is a worthy response to God, whom the Bible says loves his creation. A stress on the importance of human well-being in this present world is appropriate subjectivity in contemporary worship.

Because we are insufficient human beings, dependent upon

the architect of life for knowledge of how to live, liturgy needs to be objective. But the objectivity will be different from what we have inherited. The God we worship will not be a static entity above and beyond this world, but the dynamic, life-giving reality in all life, present in this world, acting in human history and experience. Our worship will center upon God who was, is, and will be present to life throughout the full expanse of the human story—past, present, future. If we work in harmony with that presence, heavens are realized; if we work against that presence, hell appears on earth. To believe in grace and mercy, to live by love and trust, to hope against all odds, is to affirm that life is set within an ultimate context that is trustworthy, that life does have meaning and direction. Worship that makes such an affirmation is appropriately objective and can be creative of life.

To continue to classify worship as either objective or subjective is unfortunate. As we develop new forms of worship, we ought to avoid an exclusive identity with either. The objective ground of our being and becoming is pro-human—for us—directed toward human growth and fulfillment. Our subjective, human concerns have direction only as we seek harmony with that living presence we call God.

4. An Attempt to Define Worship

Worship will fulfill its humanizing and life-giving role more readily when it is rooted where people live and search for meaning. We will see the relationship of faith to life more easily when worship probes the depths of life lived. Life will have clearer direction when worship leads us to God, who is present in the depths of existence urging us forward to the realization of human possibilities.

In other words, we must avoid defining worship exclusively in otherworldly and supernatural terms. Though worship centers upon God, it needs to be defined in a way that underscores God's presence, his action in humanizing life and building the world into his kingdom. Let us attempt such a definition.

Worship is not to engage in a sacred action separated from the ordinary circumstances of life but to encounter life and the world at the deepest level of understanding.

Worship is not to adore the Mystery of Divine Being but to wonder in the presence of mystery at the heart of life in this world.

Worship is not only to affirm "I believe in God!" but to affirm the ultimate worth of human life and the world in the presence of God, to be committed to this world and to building it into a community of peace, justice, and love.

Worship is not to look for the sacred in heavenly realms but to find the sacred in the midst of this world, to discover that life itself is a sacrament of God's presence.

Worship is not to describe what God *is* but to declare that God *acts* in human growth and becoming.

Worship is not to pay homage to a Supreme Being but in perfect freedom to respond to God's leading and participate in the process of becoming—to love, to hope, to create, to grow toward full humanity. Worship is thus to say "No!" to everything that debases and destroys human life and "Yes!" to everything that contributes to human growth and fulfillment, believing that God has the last word.

Worship is not to escape this world, to look for God at the edge of life, at the threshold of another world, but to celebrate God in the depths of this world, in mundane affairs, at the very center of life, calling us to a new future of creative possibilities.

Therefore, utilizing its rich heritage of myth and symbol, Christian worship is an *encounter* with life at its deepest level of meaning; a *celebration* of God as a dynamic, active, energizing presence at the heart of life; an *affirmation* that life has ultimate significance, for in Jesus we discover what it means to be fully human; a *response* to live a resurrection life of newness and future possibility, of growth and becoming, to take part in building a new world—a world of justice, peace, and love.

Chapter II

Guidelines
for the Development
of Liturgical Forms

To develop liturgical forms that adequately fulfill a humanizing, life-giving role is not an easy task. But nothing more crucial confronts the church. It is vital to the future of the Christian faith.

It is encouraging, therefore, that for more than a decade the church has seen great ferment in liturgical change. Numerous new official liturgies have appeared. Avant-garde liturgical celebrations have multiplied. Although these innovations have been applauded enthusiastically by some, they have been firmly resisted by others.

Change is occurring in liturgical practice, even though the goals are not always clear or the guidelines apparent. Sufficient time has now passed, however, to gain some perspective on what is happening. We can begin to anticipate in some measure the forms that liturgy may take in the decades ahead.

Most of us are now familiar with styles of celebration that are ordinarily called "experimental," "creative," or "contemporary" worship. These worship styles stress an immediacy and involvement derived largely from the insights of Marshall McLuhan. They express a more personal, intimate, and spontaneous style of worship than is generally experienced. Having little effect upon established patterns of most congregations, they usually emerge as scheduled alternatives to "traditional" worship. Advocates of the contemporary style are almost always highly critical of traditional worship.

Enough experience has been accumulated to provide us with some impressions as to the value of such worship expressions. It is clear that there are both positive and negative judgments to be made.

At its best, worship in a contemporary style brings a sense of joy to the worshiper. The way is opened for a greater utilization of the senses. Worship is more personal. It often underscores in quite forceful ways contemporary issues confronting society. It has emphasized the place of participation in worship, moving from clergy domination. It has unfolded the possibilities for the use of multifaceted media in worship. It has called in question the unduly austere formality of tradition, and has recovered the importance of persons in relationship. Whenever it is responsibly planned and carefully developed it breaks new ground and provides a glimpse of exciting possibilities for the future of worship.

However, much so-called contemporary worship tends to be thin; it is inadequate to sustain the worship life of a Christian community. While its attempt to recover the personal, intimate, and spontaneous aspects in worship has validity, the results often lack a sense of the significant, failing to touch the full dimensions of life. Therefore those qualities which sustain the greatest human growth are lacking. While the "felt" needs of some persons may appear to be met, the more important human needs that are basic to human life and spiritual development may not be met. The obsession with feeling, which often marks this worship style, seems to be little different from many forms of pietism. Theologian David Willis sees the excesses of mod worship as the "most nefarious form of this pietism." He writes:

The focus is more than ever before on the feelings of the religious devotees. . . . The symbol for this *mod pietism* would be a huge bull's eye mirror in place of the cross, so the congregation—or narcissistic audience—can "celebrate" its feelings of togetherness.[2]

The Lord's Supper, when it is celebrated in a contemporary manner, often becomes little more than a fellowship meal climaxing a rewarding group experience, thereby reinforcing the superficial theological base of much worship that is stylistically contemporary. The overwhelming stress on relating to one another in worship seems to be an overreaction to the austere, sensory-starved worship of the past.

Furthermore, a sense of historical understanding is lacking in most mod worship. Those who are responsible for such worship seldom recognize what needs to be kept that is old or what ought to be included that is new. Mod worship tends to be locked in the present, portraying an easy adjustment to contemporary culture. Because of this lack of historical sense, it tends to be ephemeral in nature, repeating the errors of the past.

There is usually an inadequate understanding of the fundamental issues of what it means to be contemporary. Such worship tends to be modern in style only. The conceptual issues of what it means to be contemporary are seldom recognized.

Apart from a rare artistic creation, most stylistically contemporary worship tends to be artistically impoverished, gimmicky, novel for the sake of novelty, carelessly conceived and poorly prepared.

When worship in a contemporary style is scheduled as a regular alternative service in a congregation, it tends also to be divisive. People divide up according to preferred styles. The "mods" in leaving the sanctuary meet the "traditionalists" as they are entering. Both groups tend to make value judgments from the perspective of their own preferred style, often making castigating remarks about the other style they avoid. This is hardly conducive to building a community of trust and support. Instead, the community is fractured, and there is no creative exchange among people through the discovery of values in both traditional and new forms and styles.

Nevertheless, the rash of "creative" worship has broken new ground. It raises issues with which all liturgical planning and development must come to grips—the utilization of the senses in worship, the church as community, participation in worship, and the relevance of worship to life. Though little of it has the quality to endure, the best of it can assist in opening up new possibilities for the future of worship.

In order that worship might adequately and responsibly fulfill its role, we need clearly established criteria by which to judge liturgical practice and develop new forms. Five guidelines seem essential. Worship must be: (1) theologically **based,** (2) historically informed, (3) relevant to human life, **(4)** artistically sensitive, and (5) appropriate to the specific congregation.

1. Worship Must Be Theologically Based

All of us who lead and shape worship need to ask, Does our worship adequately reflect the Christian faith?

Christian worship affirms and celebrates the gospel. In worship we say and act out how we believe things to be. We celebrate the meaning of life as we discern it in our faith, standing before the revelation of God. In Christian worship we renew our loyalty to Jesus Christ, recommit ourselves to ultimate values, and are given the motivational basis for all we do as Christians. Therefore, our worship is impoverished whenever it inadequately expresses the gospel.

The fundamental guideline for shaping worship is an adequately reasoned theology that is faithful to the essence of the good news of God. If it is to fulfill its God-given role, our worship must be theologically sound. When worship is theologically inadequate, the gospel is distorted. We must probe deeply into the Christian faith before we begin the task of reforming worship.

Christian worship is rooted in Christian revelation. The essence of that revelation is not ours to change. In order for Christian faith to keep relevant to contemporary life, however, we need to change our theological emphasis from time to time. We constantly need to restate the essence of the gospel in terms of modern mentality, and bring new and fresh applications of the faith to living situations. But the essence of the faith itself is constant. When by intent or careless ignorance we lose the essential nature of the gospel, we lose that which makes it *Christian* worship.

We need to take care, however, that what we affirm as the essence of the gospel is indeed the essence and not secondary issues and concerns. Theological arguments of the past too often focused on secondary matters—Biblical inerrancy, the virgin birth, the bodily resurrection of Jesus, the physical return of Jesus to the earth, a literal heaven and hell, etc. The essentials of faith, hope, love, justice, peace, as flowing from God, the ultimate source of all being, were often eclipsed. Meanings were lost in debate.

Not only must the theology that undergirds the liturgy be an adequate expression of the essence of the gospel, it must also confront contemporary life and issues. Theology that makes a difference to life will constantly be in living interaction with contemporary life. It will recognize the major human needs and issues.

A theology for contemporary worship will therefore have strong communal dimensions, recognizing that the healing and the growth of persons take place in supportive, interdependent human relationships. It will speak in the plural—communally—grasping the interrelatedness of the human family. The doctrine of the church will therefore be fundamental. It will seek to make clear the relationship of the church with the rest of the world.

A theology to undergird worship will also be missional, stressing human responsibility for the future of human life. It will give direction to human activity. It will lead to our joining God in his work in the world. It will rediscover the call of God that brought the church into being, and thereby make the purpose of the church clear. It will sense once more what it means to be in but not of the world for the sake of the world. The doctrine of creation will be important to this dimension.

Such a theology will be open to God's presence, which is at the depths of all of life. It will affirm that life has been given meaning by God. It will have a sense of cosmic inclusiveness and grandeur. The symbols of incarnation and resurrection will therefore be important, Jesus being the clue to God's working in the world. Resurrection will give assurance for hope in the face of despairing circumstances.

Such a theology will furthermore be open to the creative word that judges and redeems human life. It will address all of life as it really is, in all of its twistedness. It will speak with honesty and not illusion. The cross and the atonement will thereby find fresh interpretations.

Such a theology will have a firm vision of human possibilities in God's design and will for the world, thereby restating the doctrines of eschatology—the kingdom of God, the new age, the new creation—as the undying hope of human life.

Always at the heart of any theology that is adequate to contemporary life is the concern for the growth of persons and the becoming of the social order. Instead of taking refuge in the otherworldly, supernatural, and hierarchical, such a theology will deal creatively with human relationships and development, from the perspective of the gospel.

It is most particularly in the Lord's Supper that all these meanings find their greatest expression. The sacrament engages all of the human person. It encompasses the broadest cosmic grasp. It incorporates the undying values of myth, symbol, and ritual in elaborating Christian convictions and beliefs about life at its deepest level. The sacrament has infinite possibility for renewed meaning for all of life. Nowhere else are there such possibilities of recognizing the Beyondness in the midst of life than in the Eucharist.

It is important, therefore, that we understand that theology and liturgy are interdependent. Liturgy needs theology, and theology also needs liturgy. Without an adequately reasoned theology, worship tends to be sentimental, faddish, and subjective. But theology without liturgy tends to be pedantic and academic. Theology needs liturgy's lyrical qualities, its symbol, myth, art, and ritual. Theology needs an affirming Christian community, and the acclamations of praise that enlivens belief.

2. WORSHIP MUST BE HISTORICALLY INFORMED

In shaping liturgy, we must keep in our perspective the entire span of human history. We live in a continuum of life that has both a past and a future. How we relate to what has gone before us and how we anticipate the future are important to our self-understanding. We tend, however, to live only for the present. We have lost the skill of memory.

But memory is important to our faith. In the liturgy we recall those events of our heritage which fill life with meaning. When we reenact those events, they become a vital part of the present and contribute to our self-understanding as a Christian community.

Christian worship begins in the act of God in Jesus Christ. The church's origin, its continuing existence, and its final hope are all rooted in the Christ event. In the liturgy we proclaim and reenact those events which center in Jesus

Christ. This covenant with the past interprets the present and gives vision to the future.

We dare not allow our worship to be divorced from this communal memory. Without a sense of the past, our liturgy will live only in the vacillating and shifting views and feelings of the present. Inevitably the result is a liturgy that lacks inner resources, is superficial, trivial, and sentimental.

The fundamental corporate memories are expressed in the Scripture. Biblical events that convey to the individual the meaning and understanding of life provide the raw material for Christian worship. The representing of Scriptural events is essential to Christian worship. The acting out of the sacred story is necessary to the continuous renewal of the Christian community.

To assure the complete portrayal and reenactment of the gospel events—our origins as the people of God—it is of immeasurable value to use the lectionary and to observe the Christian year rooted in it. Their use helps overcome the narrower, limited perspective of an individual minister unaided by such a discipline. Such a practice helps us to assure that the major events of Christian origin, enriched by the contemplations of the ages, have their proper emphasis. This is essential to our self-understanding as the people of God.

Contemporary worship is impoverished if it overlooks the heritage of Christian tradition. There is great value in preserving those forms which have endured through the centuries and are a part of worship throughout Christendom.

Much tradition may be ephemeral or outmoded. But tradition has great validity when it portrays the fullness of Christian worship. In our worship we need to preserve, for example, the balance that has characterized the tradition of worship—confession, proclamation, intercession, commitment, thanksgiving. There is great value in the time-honored structure of the liturgy in which Word and sacrament are held in balance. When filled with contemporaneity, the traditional eucharistic order has great validity. It is not yet superseded. A wealth of liturgical practices and insights have been shaped into it by the people of faith down through the ages. The Eucharist links us with the believing people of God of all times and places.

Furthermore, the Eucharist is the occasion *par excellence* in which the events and meanings conveying our self-identity all converge. Christ gave us the Eucharist and it remains the brightest jewel of Christian heritage. It remains as that which most particularly characterizes Christian worship, even more than preaching or baptism.

A congregation that understandingly moves to a more frequent celebration of the Eucharist will have a firmer grasp on the meaning of the gospel, the nature and purpose of the church, and a greater feeling of at-homeness in God's universe. Any church that wants to have a clearer self-understanding ought to consider the Christian nurture that results from an enriched liturgy. The liturgy is filled with possibilities for new depth of meaning and a sense of rootedness in the continuity of life. It can, furthermore, be an antidote to the excessive subjectivity and superficiality of some current liturgical experimentation.

Using the historical norm for shaping liturgy helps us rediscover what is good in the old. That which is good and of continuing validity is preserved for the future. By keeping covenant with the past, Christian worship thereby seeks to interpret the future. We need to let valid forms of the past continue to teach us. In them we may rediscover important aspects of the Christian faith we tend to forget. By giving new life to old symbols, changeless insights into the nature of things are expressed for the new culture. Christian worship ought to use the past to learn how to build for the future. Anthropologist Margaret Mead makes this point effectively:

A good ritual is very much like a natural language. The important thing about a natural language (in contrast to a technical language created for some special purpose) is that it has been spoken for a very long time by very many kinds of people— geniuses and dullards, old people on the verge of dying and children just learning to speak, men and women, good people and bad people, farmers and scholars and fishermen. It has become a language that everyone can speak and everyone can learn, a language that carries overtones of very old meanings and the possibilities of new meanings. I think we can describe ritual in exactly the same way. It must be old, otherwise it is not polished. It must be old, otherwise it cannot reflect the play of many men's imaginations. It must be old, otherwise it will not be fully available to everyone born within the tradition. Yet it also must be alive and fresh, open to new vision and changed vision.[3]

She sees this as the very thing that the liturgical movement attempts: "to use the old symbols, but to use them with a lively, fresh insight that will free both the rituals and ourselves from the rigidity of forms that cannot contain new vision."[4]

It is important in appropriating ritual from tradition to avoid that which no longer has the ability to speak to the contemporary situation. The result of antiquated ritual is apathy and detachment. Another danger in appropriating ritual from tradition is a tendency to aestheticism which leads to a divorce of worship from the ethical dimensions of life. At the same time an impoverished ritual thwarts imagination and stifles vision.

This underscores an indispensable tension in good liturgy —a tension between valid tradition and contemporaneity. Coming to us from the past, living traditions are to be held in tension with the forms and styles of the present. To lose this tension will inevitably impoverish worship. When worship is locked in tradition, it becomes a thing belonging to the past—mere ritualism—and thereby loses life-giving qualities. But when worship practice ignores the past, superficial liturgy is inevitable, lacking a sense of rootedness in the continuity of life, and is imprisoned in the smallness of the present.

3. WORSHIP MUST BE RELEVANT TO HUMAN LIFE

Other questions important to persons who are responsible for worship are: Is the worship that is entrusted to our care creative of life? Does it speak truthfully to the depths of human life? Does it capture the wholeness of life? Worship that is adequate for its contemporary role must be relevant to human life. This criterion will ensure that theology does not become esoteric and that traditions do not become antiquarian. Contemporary worship will speak a theology in the accents of the specific time in which we live and serve. It will utilize tradition in ways that build for the future. It will stress the importance of the human, existential situation in which we daily live and work.

Worship needs to encounter this world at a level of understanding. Those fields of learning which center upon understanding human life and the world cannot be overlooked. We ignore sociology, anthropology, communications, psychology, at the peril of worship not being in touch with the way we understand ourselves and the network of relationships in which we live. Worship needs to speak with clarity and intelligibility, rejecting archaic language, speaking in contemporary accents, sensitive also to the rituals, apart from the church, by which people live.

Furthermore, worship needs to be honest and realistic so that it reflects a true image of life. Worshipers need to be encouraged to be honest rather than pretentious about life. In worship we should be able to offer our true selves, feelings, thoughts, and actions—what we are.

Good liturgy will recover the totality of human life; it will seek to overcome the tendency to divide life into sacred and secular. It will point the way to the quality of life. It will affirm everything in contemporary culture that builds life, but it will reject everything that is destructive of life and its relationships. Therefore, if worship is to contribute to contemporary living, the tension between identity with the world and detachment from the world needs to be maintained.

While recognizing the need for more personal and intimate forms of worship, contemporary worship cannot afford to lose sight of the need to recover and maintain the cosmic perspective. Only then can it speak to the larger issues that give depth to human life.

Recognizing the shift in our culture from permanence to change, those responsible for worship need both to engage in the discussions that seek to determine what is truly permanent (the very essence of the gospel) and to decide what needs to change in order to be in touch with the changes of life. The result will be that worship will be an instrument for the maturing of our theological understanding, as it maintains a dialogue with the existential situation.

Recognizing the shift in our culture from otherworldly concerns to concern for *this* life and world, those responsible for today's worship must see that it needs to reflect as much concern for the future of humankind and the world as for the past, as much concern with the human as with the godly. Worship at its best should be an encounter with the world at the deepest level of understanding.

Therefore, those who shape today's worship need to recognize their task not simply as the creative utilization of new techniques and styles, but more importantly, as being truly creative of new life. It will judge both our tendencies to secular*ism* and every form of religion that is preoccupied with the otherworldly. It will be the agent to redeem life by charting the way to the resurrection of a greater meaning through the discovery of God's presence in the depths of the ongoingness of life.

4. WORSHIP MUST BE ARTISTICALLY SENSITIVE

Worship needs to possess an artistic sensitivity. The artistic aspect of life is a valid dimension of human growth and wholeness, for it touches upon the quality of life. It is therefore tremendously important that worship have artistic sensitivity. Raimundo Panikkar, professor of religious studies at the University of California at Santa Barbara, stresses this point: "Worship has to embrace the beautiful, the true, and the good. Without a harmonious integration of these three elements human worship is always going to fall short of its nature and role."[5] Religious faith has long called forth the very best art to express faith.

This criterion encourages the use of the many possible forms of artistic expression—the physical setting of worship, the way the thematic focus is developed, how worship coheres, the skill with which liturgy is done.

With the great variety of communicative methods available today, the possibilities of artistic expression are greatly amplified. Much "experimental worship" focuses upon new media techniques. When these are carefully planned, mature in expression, theologically sound, well executed, and not excessively iconoclastic, the utilization of the many media techniques can be effective. They enable less dependence upon verbal expression and can recover a sense of involvement, movement, and occasionally artistic integrity.

Great care needs to be taken in the use of various media techniques. Many are powerful and can so dominate everything else that they become ends in themselves.

Showmanship is to be avoided, with a careful distinction being made between worship and entertainment. Unless this distinction is made, the spectator role in worship is inevitably perpetuated. The need in worship is to be sensory without being sensational, to use new forms without being gimmicky.

With the emerging of a greater involvement of the people in worship, care needs to be taken to avoid mediocrity, without developing the spirit of professionalism and clericalism. The best artistic expression still is to be cherished, and a standard of excellence maintained, regardless of the particular artistic style or form that is utilized. It is important also to incorporate artistic styles that convey timeliness. Such forms reflect contemporary awareness that greatly aids worship in possessing a quality of relevance to the issues of our day.

Good art lifts worship above the casual and ordinary. God in Jesus Christ opened the way to unlimited possibilities for human life. That event is filled with ultimate meaning for human existence. The magnitude of this concept, to be adequately conveyed in worship, requires an eloquence, a "grand" style. To this end, good art helps to avoid the dullness, monotony, and flatness that stifle the fullest expression of the meaning of worship. Raimundo Panikkar stresses this when he states: "Any act of worship should be a deepening of our feelings, an awareness of the tremendous weight of everything. From this point of view, worship could be described as those acts by which we express our stepping out of the banal."[6] Even though the personal and intimate qualities are important recoveries in contemporary worship, the cosmic sense which good art helps worship to maintain must not be lost.

Though rarely achieved in "experimental" worship, new communicative means possess great potential to convey a sense of occasion, to underscore the vast meanings of life, to overcome the smallness of so much of our living. Good art can thus help to convey a sense of the significant.

Artistic sensitivity recognizes that worship uses a language different from that in which moderns easily converse.

Christian worship uses the language of myth, symbol, and ritual in speaking about the depths of reality. No other alternative is adequate to the task of human self-understanding at its deepest level than a mature use of such language, utilized in a way appropriate for today's setting. To fail to recognize the artistic aspect of life is to fail to utilize that which can most effectively touch the deepest levels of life.

5. WORSHIP MUST BE APPROPRIATE TO THE SPECIFIC CONGREGATION

It is likewise important that contemporary worship be appropriate to the particular community of people who worship together. Therefore we need to ask, Is our worship appropriate to the particular people who are engaged in it?

Contemporary worship, if it is to have a positive role, needs to have a direct relationship to the life of the worshiping community. It cannot live exclusively on an ethereal level above the people. It needs to be localized, reflecting the needs and the level of maturity of the specific congregation.

Contemporary worship will also respect the variety of persons who comprise a typical congregation. Modern life is characterized by a pluralism not known in prior centuries. A flexibility therefore needs to mark worship. Those who shape worship need to learn to speak in different accents, engaging people in their differences. While worship must remain faithful to the essentials, a variety of styles and forms in ever-changing circumstances need to be encouraged. There is much value in utilizing the variety of liturgical expressions that are available. The result in practice is a kind of mosaic or collage style of worship. An eclectic approach has much in its favor.

Care should be taken to avoid fractionalizing a congregation into different groups that have little interaction. This happens when congregations foster "contemporary," "guitar," "rock," or "youth" services regularly at one hour and "traditional" worship at another. There is too much value in both contemporary and inherited styles to allow people to become confined within one or the other. A mosaic approach has the greater value in that it speaks creatively to all. It opens up possibilities of an ever-widening appreciation of new and unfamiliar forms and styles. It reveals the need for people with varying appreciations to open up to one another, and prevents the domination of any particular preference.

While worship needs to have a localized expression, a congregation is not served well if it becomes provincial. Worship must focus on the needs of a specific people without losing a sense of relatedness with the whole human family. Worship must reflect the needs and the level of maturity of a specific congregation, but must also keep clearly in view where they ought to be. Worship needs to address the living issues of specific persons and their community, but should never lose a perspective on the broader issues of the larger communities that make up society. Thus, worship will need to speak in terms that appropriately express the life of a specific people in the total context of their life. This is most important if the worship of a given people is supportive of their missional responsibilities.

This tension between the local and the universal is important to the growth of persons and to the development of human relationships. It recognizes where we are as a people, but also recognizes where we ought to be, and is not content unless there is movement from where we are to where we can be. It is in this tension that questions of pastoral responsibility are to be raised and answered. We must ask: When is it, and when is it not, a responsible act to change familiar and meaningful liturgical forms, and introduce the new and unfamiliar? When is it justified to destroy frames of reference that for some still have great meaning but for others are outmoded?

It is certain that Christian faith must move toward mature expression. But the decision as to how fast is pastorally responsible is a decision to be made in the light of a given local situation. While it often may seem easier and less traumatic to move slowly, there is an urgency about the Christian witness in the world. Crucial issues that affect present and future life must be addressed by a maturing Christian faith and mission. For those in touch with life in the world, much of what the church continues to say and do has already lost its force. The task, then, for those who shape worship is in large measure that of building the new out of the wreckage of the old. At times pastoral responsibility may mean helping some persons to relate to a different congregation that more adequately meets their needs as they understand them, recognizing that no single congregation can effectively serve every person and every felt need.

The ultimate test of worship is the extent to which a congregation moves out of its introversion and engages in mission in social structures. What does the church do in the world *after* worship?

Worship is at the very heart of the church's life. It expresses the nature of its life together, as it discovers that life in Christ. From it flows the church's missional activity in the world. No issue confronting the church today is more crucial than the development of a truly contemporary and life-building worship. Guidelines such as these perhaps can assist a congregation to maintain a worship style that can release the creative energy of the Christian faith for living in these times.

Chapter III

The Centrality
of the
Lord's Supper

The worship of the church lies at the very heart of church life. It is the creative center of the whole life of the people of God—both in their life together and in their involvement in God's mission in the world. The church's worship is both the summit of the church's life together and the fountain from which the church's power flows.

The eucharistic celebration therefore has great life-giving potential. The Lord's Supper is the fullest expression of Christian worship given by Jesus Christ himself for the continuing nurture of the church. From the very beginning of the church's existence, and throughout the centuries, this sacrament has been the principal source of Christian nurture. There is nothing older in all Christendom. Before the first word of the New Testament was written, before any creeds were formed, before churchly structures were established, the celebration of the Eucharist was at the very heart of Christian faith and life.

Nevertheless, for many today, the Lord's Supper no longer seems to have roots in life as it is lived. It often seems alien to contemporary experience, and culturally dead. Perhaps the reason is that the sacrament has become peripheral in our religious life. Perhaps it is that we observe it so infrequently that we are limited in our understanding of its meaning and have failed to find those cultural roots which would give the sacrament a truly contemporary relevance. New theological emphases will help to restore its relevance for us and assist us in recognizing that the Lord's Supper does touch life at its deepest level. Fresh perspectives on the sacrament can possibly once more provide depth to contemporary life.

1. THE NATURE OF SACRAMENT

The Holiness of the Ordinary. The sacraments use very ordinary things of life. In Baptism, it is water. In the Lord's Supper, it is bread and wine. The very essence of sacrament is to take the ordinary and make it a sign of the presence of God. This is the nature of sacrament. The common, ordinary stuff of every life is given sacred depth. In the Lord's Supper, God is known in the ordinary circumstances of the Christian community gathered about a table engaged in the commonplace act of breaking bread and sharing a cup.

There is an incarnational aspect in this sacrament of "Word made flesh." In this common act an "enfleshment" of the sacred occurs. The Beyond is recognized in the fabric of everyday life. The common is charged with the grandeur of God. The ordinary and the extraordinary, the secular and the sacred, politics and prayer, are united. God is known in the ordinary and commonplace.

Presence. The nature of the Lord's Supper as sacrament has throughout the centuries focused primarily upon a doctrine of Real Presence—that Christ is in some manner present and operative in the sacrament. Debate has centered upon the question, How is Christ present? Views have ranged from the transubstantiation of Roman Catholics to the memorialism of Zwingli. In the Roman view, against which the Reformers reacted, the symbol and that which the symbol signified were merged into one. This led to an understanding of presence that was actualized, localized spatially, in the elements of bread and wine themselves. For Zwingli, the sacrament was a commemoration, a thanksgiving for what Christ did, the bread and the wine were "naked and bare signs." The view of Zwingli was equally opposed by Calvin and other dominant leaders of the Reformation.

For Calvin, the sacrament was the instrument, or means of grace, whereby all that the sacrament signifies is communicated to the communicant. This view of Presence, which is the basis of all the confessional statements of the Reformed tradition, centers on the understanding that the sacrament is a present offering of the gospel itself. In the sacrament, Christ is active in the present. Christ gives, not merely gave. We receive, not merely remember that he once gave.

From the perspective of sacrament giving sacred depth to the common, ordinary stuff of life, the doctrine of Presence ought to have a broader meaning than it ordinarily has had. Christ's presence in the sacrament ought to symbolize his presence in all of life. Anglican bishop John A. T. Robinson points out that the doctrine of the Real Presence when attached exclusively to the bread and wine has "disincarnated the Christ from 'common flesh' and banished him from lower-case living." Though it was not the intent of the church fathers, the effect "has been to do the one thing the Fathers most feared: *solvere Christum,* to make him a dissociated personality, with the *divinum* cut off from the *humanum.*"[7]

In the sacrament we experience that Presence which indwells all reality—a Presence not by exclusion (that this Presence is known only here and nowhere else), but by inclusion (that his presence here is a sign of his presence everywhere). The Roman Catholic Vatican II document *The Constitution on the Sacred Liturgy* rather effectively broadens the doctrine of Real Presence to other aspects of worship:

Christ is always present in His Church, especially in her liturgical celebrations. He is present in the sacrifice of the Mass, not
only in the person of His minister, . . . but especially under the
Eucharistic species. By His power He is present in the sacraments, so that when a man baptizes it is really Christ Himself
who baptizes. He is present in His word, since it is He Himself
who speaks when the holy Scriptures are read in the church. He
is present, finally, when the Church prays and sings, for He
promised: "Where two or three are gathered together for my
sake, there am I in the midst of them" (Mt. 18:20).[8]

The presence we affirm in the sacrament we affirm for the
entire liturgical act, even the entire life of the community in
its varied activities.

Moreover, what we come to know here gives us insight
into the rest of reality. In this particular assembling of the
people of God, breaking bread together, we come to know
that there is an indwelling presence in all of our breaking of
bread together—in all of our relationships, all of history, all
of reality. There is a living Presence in the depths of everything.

Christians worship God in a specific place and at a specific
time, not implying by such acts that God is excluded from
all other times and places, but making clear that what is true
of this time and place is true of all times and places—that all
reality is indwelt. In fact, we need to know this presence in
just such a specific way in the sacrament if we are to realize
that same presence in the rest of reality. It is questionable
whether we can understand that all reality is indwelt, if that
indwelling is not regularly celebrated in a specific and more
localized manner. Just as Jesus Christ is the clue to how God
is at work in every time and every place, so the sacrament
points to the world, the ordinary relationships of life, as the
scene of God's work in our midst. We come to realize that
everything is dependent upon the steadfast love, grace, and
trustworthiness of God.

The recovery of the centrality of the sacrament therefore ought not to be seen as being *more* confined to the sanctuary, to a narrowly religious sphere, *more* withdrawn from the concerns of worldly life. Rather, it is intended to help us gain a perspective that recognizes, in the depths of all life, a sacred presence that draws all life toward its fulfillment. So the sacrament points us to the world, the ordinary things and relationships, as the scene of God's work in our midst. It reminds us of the immanence of God in the depths of creation, active in all of life's relationships, just as God acted in Jesus of Nazareth. His presence here is a sign of his presence everywhere. Knowing his presence in the life of the community becomes a symbol of that presence in all of reality.

The recovery of the centrality of the sacrament therefore ought to help us gain a perspective that recognizes a sacred presence in all of life, that draws all of life toward the realization of its possibilities. May we begin to see in the gathering of Christians about a table, eating bread and drinking wine, the sacrament of God's presence and discover a world transparent to the God who in its depths is creating all things new, who in the midst of human relationships is reconciling, restoring, healing, working for peace, justice, and freedom.

2. WORD AND SACRAMENT

The early church celebrated this sacrament on each Lord's Day. It was an indispensable part of Christian worship. In the sixteenth century, the Protestant Reformers insisted that the norm of Christian worship was the weekly celebration of the sacrament which included the preaching of the Word. The reformed liturgical ideal focused upon both Word and sacrament, rather than allowing either to be magnified at the expense of the other. For John Calvin, it was the same Word whether coming through Scripture, sermon, or sacrament. Whereas the sermon and Scripture were the Word spoken and heard, the sacraments were the Word in visible form, graphically representing God's promises. Together, sermon, Scripture, and sacrament were the vehicles of Christ's presence.

However, Calvin was never permitted to practice the unity of Word and sacrament to the extent that he sought. It has rarely been fully realized in Protestantism. The sermon, with its verbal and intellectual emphasis, came to dominate. The sacrament was eclipsed through infrequent observance. Consequently, Protestant worship is generally thought to be primarily a preaching service—the sermon the distinctive and invariable feature.

It was perhaps the invention of the printing press and the resultant focus upon words that had much to do with Protestantism's focus upon the Word. Furthermore, there has always tended to be a confusion between words and Word in Protestant worship. The verbal has even dominated within the sacramental acts. James F. White states: "Protestant emphasis on verbal communication has distorted the sacraments so that they are underacted and overarticulated."[9]

While it may have been the neglect of the sacrament that led to an overly intellectualized kind of worship within the Protestant tradition, more likely it was the overly intellectual, with its verbal focus, that led to the neglect of the sacrament. In either case, worship that is overly intellectualized, overly verbal, finds little room for sacrament.

It may be that the contemporary change in which our culture is developing a more sensory awareness of life and its environment is contributing to the recovery of an appreciation of the sacrament. The sacrament is more sensory than the Word/words-dominated worship which we have inherited.

Although the unity of Word and sacrament still rarely finds expression among Protestants, the sacrament is beginning to be recognized as central to worship and deserving of a place equal to Word written and preached. Conversely, among Roman Catholics, who for centuries neglected the Word written and preached, a recovery of the importance of Scripture and preaching is taking place.

This growing emphasis on the centrality of both Word and sacrament among Protestants is underscored in the United Presbyterian Directory for the Worship of God. The Directory defines the Word of God in the following way: "The Word of God is essentially Jesus Christ. . . . All particular acts of worship receive their significance as they relate to what God has done, is doing, and will do, in Jesus Christ."[10] This understanding of the Word is proclaimed and manifested in worship "through Scripture, sermon, and sacrament," through which "the incarnate Word of God, Jesus Christ, becomes contemporary for his people, a true and living Word, addressed to them, and demanding their response."[11] Scripture, sermon, and sacrament are then described as "written Word," "preached Word," and "the visible Word of the sacraments." It states, "As in the written and preached Word, so in the sacraments Jesus Christ is present with his people. . . . The sacraments are an essential part of the public ministry of the Church, in which all Christians are expected to participate."[12]

Calvin's insistence upon the centrality of the Lord's Supper in the worship of each Lord's Day is reechoed in this statement: "It is fitting that it be observed as frequently as on each Lord's Day, and it ought to be observed frequently and regularly enough that it is seen as a proper part of, and not an addition to, the worship of God by his people."[13]

3. The Lord's Supper as Response

Christian worship embodies both the action of God and the response of the people. But it is God who takes the initiative, and our worship is a response to God's initiative.

God speaks! We reply! In worship, the acts and presence of God in the midst of human life and history are made known and we in turn respond by giving ourselves to God for his purpose. Worship is therefore a response—an expression of our conviction that God is present to human life here and now.

True Christian worship therefore needs to focus first of all upon God. Too often it is not so. Much so-called Christian worship is self-centered, evidenced by many of the songs that are frequently sung by Christians. God is in truth the great subject of worship. As that point in life where the highest of life's values and the bigger meanings are celebrated, worship centers upon God the source of meaning and value. Its consequences for human life are therefore derivative—the result of worship's God-centeredness.

The action of God and the response of the people is most clearly seen in the fourfold action of the Eucharist, based upon the actions of Jesus at the Last Supper (Mark 14:22–23). Jesus *took* bread and the cup, *gave thanks, broke* the bread, and *gave* it to his disciples. He took, gave thanks, broke, and gave—offering, thanksgiving, breaking of bread, and eating.

These four acts parallel the ordinary acts of a common meal. First, the table is set, the table grace is spoken, the food is given its final preparation for serving, and lastly the food is eaten.

The Offering. The offering is the first action of the Lord's Supper—"he *took* bread . . . he *took* a cup." As stewards of God's gifts to us, we give bread and wine—symbols of our whole selves—in grateful response to God's great gifts to us.

There is nothing more basic to human existence than food and drink. The power of the sacrament to touch our lives lies here. The sacramental food and drink suggest all that is essential to sustain human life. Life depends on continuous nourishment from food and drink. The bread and the wine also suggest all that gives life joy as well. Good food and drink are essential to the joyous celebrations of living, especially when shared with family and friends.

Both the bread and the wine are products of human toil using the raw materials of wheat and grapes. In the manufacture of bread and wine the whole complex of industrial and commercial life is involved—agriculture, research, genetics, engineering, transportation, machine processing, business. Involved also are the sins of society—selfishness, abuse, greed, waste, and injustice. All of this—our whole political, social, and economic order—is offered in the bread and wine. This meaning needs to be brought home to worshipers, for it points up a vital aspect of the relationship of the sacrament to daily affairs.

The procession of gifts to the holy table therefore starts in the midst of everyday life—our family dining table; the factory, office, classroom, laboratory, legislature, or store where we work; the place of our leisure. In response to God's initiative we give ourselves to God, that he may get his hands on that part of the world which we represent, to the end that the whole world may be changed. We are the loaves and small fish which God seeks to use to perform the miracle of a new creation—the kingdom of God.

The offering thus points forward to the new creation, the kingdom of God. The Eucharist is given cosmic dimensions. The farthest reaches of human existence—all creation, all history and event, all people, all things, every aspiration for good, the whole cosmic sweep—are offered to God, for all that is, is encompassed within the redemptive design of God. To know the scope of God's design, which is focused in the Eucharist, should help us overcome every sense of smallness or provincialism in doing liturgy.

The Thanksgiving. The thanksgiving is the second action of the Lord's Supper. "He took bread, and *blessed* . . . he took a cup" and *gave thanks.* Just as Jesus gave thanks over the bread and wine of the Last Supper, so do we.

The table is set. We pray the family's table grace over the bread and wine. Gathered as the family of God, the church thanks God, in the manner of the Jewish table blessings from which the prayer derives, for his great mercies.

This prayer is the greatest act of praise in all of Christian liturgy. This prayer gives the sacrament its character, for the Greek word for "thanksgiving" *(eucharistia)* very early gave the sacrament its name—the Eucharist (i.e., the thanksgiving).

The prayer of thanksgiving recalls God's mighty acts and unites the worshipers with the whole family of God throughout all ages, all nations and peoples and tongues, with the whole company of heaven and earth. Thanks is given especially for the gift of Jesus Christ. Time—past, present, future—is spanned as Christ's coming in flesh is recalled, his coming into our midst is welcomed, his coming again as the kingdom is awaited. The Spirit of God is invoked to ensure that what is done is by the grace of God, and that we may be bound together as a people in Christ. The prayer climaxes as we offer ourselves as members of Christ's body to be used as God's agents in the world.

As a family made one in Christ, we then pray together the family prayer of the people of God—the Lord's Prayer. Once more, we yield ourselves to God's ordering by hallowing his name, and by pledging to do his will. The Lord's Prayer thus crowns the second action of the Lord's Supper.

The Breaking of Bread. The breaking of the bread is the third action of the Lord's Supper. "He took bread, and blessed, and *broke it* . . ." The bread is broken in order that it may be eaten. It has the same purpose as slicing a loaf at meals, or breaking a particularly savory loaf at a simple picnic. A single loaf declares the unity of the mystical body of Christ, emphasizing what Paul wrote: "Because there is one loaf, we, many as we are, are one body; for it is one loaf of which we all partake" (I Cor. 10:17, NEB).

Other symbolic meanings are associated with the action. The breaking of bread and the pouring of the wine show forth the cost of human redemption, that Christ's body was broken and his life was poured out on the cross.

The Eating. Eating is the fourth action of the Lord's Supper. "He took bread, and blessed, and broke it, and *gave* it to them. . . . And he took a cup, and when he had given thanks he *gave* it to them, and they all drank of it."

Just as the early Christians believed that the resurrected Christ continued to be present with them as they ate the Lord's Supper together, so we should understand that in this meal we are joined together with the risen Christ. "Where two or three are gathered in my name, there am I in the midst of them" (Matt. 18:20).

But the sacrament is a communion not only with the Christ but with one another also. The meal is not a private devotion. It is a family affair, a banquet in which all share together.

This communal understanding is important, for in this meal we catch a glimpse of a world re-created by Christ— the new creation. We see what we ought to be, and are reminded of the kind of world God wills.

The pattern of the eucharistic response is that we are taken as we are, in order that we and our world may be made what we are not—as God desires. In celebrating the sacrament, we are renewed in the meaning that God gives to life.

4. THE ROLE OF THE EUCHARIST IN FORMING THE CHURCH

It is most particularly in the assembling of the people of God in worship that the church is created. In worship the church turns to the source and object of its identity and acknowledges the supremacy of Christ over all of life. Here the people are formed once again as the church. This is most clearly seen in the celebration of the Eucharist, for in the Eucharist the Christian community manifests its true life together in fellowship with its Lord and celebrates the covenant that constitutes it.

The early Christians clearly understood that it was their worship together that made them the church. Even though the Roman government considered the assembling for Christian worship a crime punishable by death, the early Christians regarded worship as indispensable. To be absent from the worshiping fellowship was to separate from the body of Christ. It is this understanding which prompted John A. T. Robinson to write that we come to the Eucharist "not merely to feed upon the Body of Christ, but to be created the Body of Christ."[14]

The Body of Christ. An adequate understanding of the nature of the sacrament depends upon an adequate understanding of the nature of the church. Eucharist and church together share the essential meaning of the gospel.

Paul emphasized that Christian experience centers upon a life that is "in Christ." To be in Christ was to be "a member of the body of Christ." To be a member of the body of Christ was to be in Christ. The two were identical in his theology.

Since the love of God became a definitive event in Jesus Christ, love is the essential quality of life in Christ. The church, as the body of Christ, is to be a fellowship marked by love—love of God and love of fellow human beings. A caring, deeply concerned, and self-giving love should lead the Christian community into an ever-expanding fellowship that moves into a growing concern that embraces the world.

The body of Christ might therefore be termed the body of Love. ("Love" is capitalized to make clear that it refers to God, who is the personification of universal, cosmic love.) If the church is without any mark of love, it surely does not deserve to be called the body of Christ. The essence and glory of the church is that it is to be the body of Christ—the body of Love. But when it fails to be this, it fails to be its true self. To be the body of Christ—the body of Love—is the unique nature of the church in spite of the human defects and limitations that often tend to obliterate that nature.

Although the church is meant to be the body of Christ, it is to be clearly understood that what God wills the church to be, God wills all creation to be. The church is what it is by *in*clusion, rather than by *ex*clusion—inclusion of all that is, rather than exclusion of all that is not the church. The church is therefore meant to be a symbol that every aspect of life, of all time, to the farthest reaches of the universe are to be the body of Christ—the body of Love. The celebration of the Eucharist may properly encompass all that it means to be the body of Christ.

Covenant. Because the Eucharist is the celebration of the establishment of the new covenant of God with his people, the Eucharist is most particularly the occasion when the church as the community of God is reconstituted.

The words of institution (from Paul), spoken by the liturgical celebrant at each Eucharist, state: "This cup is the new covenant sealed by my blood" (I Cor. 11:25, NEB); and "every time you eat this bread and drink the cup, you proclaim the death of the Lord, until he comes" (I Cor. 11:26, NEB). It is clear that for Paul, at least, the celebration of the sacrament related Christ's followers to Jesus' crucifixion.

Because the sacrament seems to be narrowly attached to Jesus' death, and to particular doctrines of the atonement and to "blood," the Eucharist tends to lack meaning for many people. The continued use of the traditional words of institution therefore requires a fresh understanding. The celebration should not be exclusively identified with Jesus' death, even though that is a part of its meaning. It is important to remember that every eucharistic celebration from the beginning of Christian history has been since the resurrection of

Jesus. The Eucharist therefore views Jesus' death from the
perspective of resurrection. The Eucharist is primarily a resurrection fellowship. Furthermore, the sacrament is in reality
a celebration of the whole Christ event as revealed in Jesus
—birth-life-ministry-death-resurrection-ascension-coming
again.

Nevertheless Christians have found in the cross/resurrec-
tion motif the essence of the meaning of the Christ event and
therefore the meaning of the gospel. Most particularly in the
cross we discover the work of Love creating a new community—a new humanity—out of the twisted human situation.
In the cross we understand that God does not allow even
human sin to thwart his desire to move his creation toward
the wholeness he wills. In the cross we come to recognize that
wherever we see God's love transforming the disfigured life
of humanity, we witness the work of God which was most
particularly evidenced in Jesus. Involving both God's activity
and the human response, atonement leads to new community. Brought into being by Love that suffers and forgives, the
quality of the life of this new community is based on God's
work of reconciliation—remembered, experienced, and an-
ticipated. This work of Love, creating a new humanity out
of the fallen human situation, is of the essence of the new
covenant celebrated in the Eucharist.

This covenant was sealed with blood, as the words of
institution inform us. The idea of a covenant being sealed
with blood is a difficult concept for us, perhaps the most
difficult of all symbols. It reflects the ancient understanding
that blood effected the establishment of communal relationships of God and his people. For example, in the constituting
of the old covenant, Moses took animal blood and threw half
of it against the altar. He then read the book of the covenant.
The people responded by pledging their obedience to the
covenant. Then Moses threw the rest of the blood upon the

people (Ex. 24:6–8). The covenant was sealed, confirmed, ratified, with blood.

It was natural therefore for the *new* covenant to be sealed with blood. The early Christians understood this, for it held a common meaning for them. They came to see, therefore, Jesus' crucifixion—his blood—as just this ratification of a new covenant. It is important, however, to recognize that the emphasis is really not upon blood but is upon covenant. Here we become confused. The blood had the secondary role of sealing, of confirming, of ratifying the covenant. It was the covenant that was all-important: "This cup is the new covenant sealed by my blood." It was a kind of signing the covenant with a signature of blood.

Whereas the old covenant centered upon a written law, the new covenant centers upon the spirit of love. Whereas the old covenant was established with Israel, the new covenant is meant for all humankind. It is a universal covenant. The Christ event transforms Jewish history into world history.

Therefore, in drinking this cup—the cup of the covenant —we affirm the importance of the Jesus event, and agree to let our lives be shaped by it. We affirm that the Jesus event will be for us the center of the meaning of life, that it will play a significant role in the way we look upon the events and circumstances of the world.

In sharing this sacrament we are covenanted to one another in Christ. In drinking this cup we accept responsibility for one another and thus express the relational dimensions of the covenant. We become responsible for one another and for all. Each sharing of the cup renews the contract between ourselves and God, and shapes the style of our relationships in life.

The Eucharist thus sums up the meaning of the gospel, and affirms the reality of that Love which was made known in the Christ. In this sacrament we are re-created the new community—the body of Christ—the body of Love. In the cup of the new covenant we thus celebrate the inauguration of the rule of God among humankind through the Christ, and we affirm his continued involvement in humankind to bring the kingdom to fulfillment.

5. THE COMMUNAL NATURE OF HOLY COMMUNION

We are most fully human when in community. We do not fully realize the wholeness of our humanity alone. To be human is to be in relationship. Growth occurs in interpersonal relationships. This understanding is implicit in the communal dimensions of the church and its liturgy, for Christian worship is essentially communal. In the sacrament we gather at the table as the family of faith and love.

Persons in Community. Love is most especially a communal thing. One cannot really love in isolation from others. If love is indeed a part of the meaning of human life, and an aspect of human wholeness, then to keep to oneself betrays human nature and stunts personal development.

A person does not come to know God and others in isolation. We are called through and into a community—the community of faith and love—the church. To be a Christian is to be part of that people whom God has bound together. From our life together within this community of faith, we derive our fulfillment as individual Christians, and find meaning and direction.

The church, then, is not merely a collection of individuals, but is a community, a living organism, a social solidarity. Just as a family is something more than a group of individuals, so also is the church.

It is important to note that in this communal relationship, the person is not merely submerged into group or mass. In true community the needs of the person are met and the individual finds fulfillment, persons are treated as persons rather than objects. Love, mutual support, and caring bind the community together.

Such a community is the only valid form of community. It protests against selfish individualism, but it also protests against every form of communal life that absorbs or submerges the person into a faceless mass, or that exhibits, diminishes, or otherwise tends to destroy one's personhood.

Based upon this understanding of the communal nature of all human life and the Christian faith, the Lord's Supper is essentially communal. It is the family meal of the people of God and is not individualistic in nature. The tendency to lose oneself in private devotions in the sacrament is contrary to the understanding that we are eating a meal together with other people. Any meal eaten together is a social experience. In the sacred meal, the communicant is united with the entire fellowship. At the Lord's Table we are not like a gathering of individual diners in a restaurant, but are a family gathered together. Here the people are sustained in the fellowship of the body of Christ. Here the believing community derives its life from a source beyond itself, and is renewed in fellowship with the risen Lord. In the Lord's Supper is to be found the unity in Christ which alone enables us to say, "we."

Liturgist Scott Francis Brenner aptly summarizes this understanding:

A Christian is one who responds to the word of God in Jesus Christ, is baptized in the Lord and is delivered from his aloneness and made one member of a *koinonia,* a fellowship, gathered about a table. This basic concept of fellowship, of community, is the heart of our faith, and indicates that God plans to save his people from self-destruction through community and communion. The more we think of that one table and the worldwide family gathered about it, the more we must exult, "Here is a faith for our time!"[15]

The assembled congregation is as important to the sacrament as are the bread and wine. As a sacrament of relationships, the community itself is as much one of the elements of the sacrament as are the bread and wine.

In a text cited above, Paul underscored this unity when he wrote to the Corinthians:

> When we bless "the cup of blessing," is it not a means of sharing in the blood of Christ? When we break the bread, is it not a means of sharing in the body of Christ? Because there is one loaf, we, many as we are, are one body; for it is one loaf of which we all partake. (I Cor. 10:16–17, NEB)

The Sacrament of Unity. The Eucharist celebrates the social nature of humankind. It celebrates the reality that all life, all meaning, is communal. Therefore, this communal understanding of the family of God gathered at the table contains the seed of social concern. For at the table the many are made into a unity. Here is the "new creation." God intends that this community be an expression in microcosm of that which God desires the whole community of humankind to be—a community of reconciliation. Here "there is neither Jew nor Greek . . . slave nor free . . . male nor female" (Gal. 3:28). The unity that is to be actualized in the sacrament demonstrates God's plan for the unity of all creation— all races, all nationalities, all tongues, all classes. No divisiveness can be tolerated at the table if the communal nature of the sacrament is accepted. It thus embraces that hope which envisions the removal of all barriers that keep humankind from realizing its essential unity. That which we come to know at the holy table we seek to realize in all society.

When this communal, unifying basis of the sacrament is understood, "a person cannot go to the Eucharist to escape the world's problems; he can go there, however, to escape the world's answers."[16]

Biblical scholar Norman Perrin has provided a helpful

study of Scriptural sources. In it he argues that the communal sacramental meals of earliest Christianity were an expression of the table fellowship of Jesus not only with the good
and respectable but also with "tax collectors and sinners"—
the social outcasts. Jesus' table fellowship ignored religious
convention and social distinction. This had great meaning for
Jesus' followers but was offensive to his critics. Perrin maintains that Jesus' followers wished to perpetuate this ideal of
unity in fellowship, in the sacramental meal. The table fellowship of Jesus was seen as an anticipation of the messianic
feast to be expected in the kingdom—a feast of unity. Perrin
suggests that it was therefore a kind of acted parable of the
kingdom of God. Early Christian communal meals, he states,
were recognized as a continuation of this regular practice of
Jesus' ministry, and symbolized the kind of relationship
made possible by the common acceptance of the challenge.[17]

It is probable that the failure of the Corinthians properly
to "discern the Body" (I Cor. 11:29, NEB) was a failure to
express this unifying kind of fellowship. The Corinthian
church was troubled by divisions. The Corinthians failed to
demonstrate what it meant to be the body of Christ by offend-
ing the poorer ones among them. For Paul the unity of the
church as the body of Christ was symbolized in the sacramental loaf, of which Jesus, according to tradition, said,
"This is my body" (I Cor. 11:24). Therefore, "any one who
eats and drinks without discerning the body" (i.e., the
"church" as an organic, unified body) "eats and drinks judgment upon himself" (I Cor. 11:29). This failure to live in
koinonia, that is, to live in love and supportive communal
relationships at the Table of the Lord became judgment. By
ignoring the needs of the lesser privileged, and by their selfish
exclusion of them, they failed to fulfill their true nature as the
church—the body of Christ—made one by the spirit of love.

Thus the Eucharist, in celebrating the social nature of
humankind, expresses the hope of reconciliation among all

people, in which all barriers between people are broken down.

Participation. Another aspect of the communal nature of the church, and thus of its worship, is the doctrine of the priesthood of all believers. The body of Christ is a priestly body. Too often this doctrine, important to the Reformers, is interpreted in a way that makes it a priesthood of *each* believer. The Reformers did not have such an individualistic concept in mind. This doctrine is as communal as the metaphor of the body of Christ. It is the priesthood of *all* believers.

The liturgy is therefore something done by the whole priestly body. A great diversity of gifts exists within the community. These are to be used for the building up of the whole body (Rom., ch. 12; I Cor., ch. 12; Eph., ch. 4; I Peter 4:10f.). Every member of a congregation needs to understand and value his or her particular role and that of others. If this potential for service could be fully realized, the church's total life would be transformed. The whole church would be revitalized in both its liturgy and its mission in the world.

Christian worship is too often seen as something performed by the clergy for the benefit of the laity, the worshiper being little more than a spectator. Worship tends to become passive when a sense of participation in a communal action is missing. Roman Catholic theologian Charles Davis states: "The church is not a theater but a house. It is a family that is gathered together, not an audience. The people are there to take part, not to watch."[18]

True Christian worship is an act of the whole people—clergy and laity together. For example, prayer in worship is *common* prayer—prayer that the whole community offers *in common.* When the minister prays alone, he or she represents the whole congregation, and is not simply engaging in personal prayer to which the laity are expected to listen passively.

This sense of the communal participation is expressed by James F. White as a need to amateurize worship: "Worship is a do-it-yourself job not surrogated to others." He states, "Recovering the amateur status of worship is essentially recovering a proper doctrine of the Church as consisting of the laity as much as the clergy."[19] All have a role to play in the liturgy, although the roles will vary according to gifts and office.

The word "liturgy" derives from the Greek word *leitourgia* and is formed from two words, *laos,* meaning "people," and *ergon,* meaning "work." The literal meaning of *leitourgia* is therefore "the work of the people," and in ancient Greece denoted the performance of some public responsibility by Greek citizens. When applied to the life of the Christian community it means the work of the people gathered to glorify and praise God. But it also has a wider meaning extending beyond the corporate gathering as the work of the people in the life of the world. Liturgy thus involves the total work of the people in the service of God.

6. IN THE EUCHARIST, THE MERGING OF PAST AND FUTURE INTO THE PRESENT

Judeo-Christian faith takes time and history seriously. It is a faith that affirms that God is the source, guide, and goal of all history. God has acted, and will act in renewing all things. Past and future—memory and hope—are therefore important. In the liturgy, especially in the Eucharist, we identify with that people of faith who across the ages have lived out of the past into the future.

The Eucharist and the Continuity of the People of God. The church lives within a heritage of history. Conscious of the transitoriness of life, the church experiences the continuity of its worship through the centuries, and senses its union with the church of all ages. This continuity with the past is an important aspect of the church's self-understanding. The church cannot fully know itself apart from its history.

This believing, continuing tradition provides the principal source for awakening our own belief. We believe today because we have found a place within a tradition of faith—a tradition that was here long before we came along and that will be here long after we are gone. Our faith is a living part of that long continuum which began with a people who were conscious of God's activity in the midst of their own experience. Passing from Exodus through the occasions of fidelity to God and wanderings from God, we can trace the story of the people of God. That story for us culminates in Jesus the Christ. We are "built upon the foundation of the apostles and prophets, Christ Jesus himself being the cornerstone" (Eph. 2:20). Continuing through two millennia of post-Biblical history, millions today, living within this heritage, find a light to illumine some of the puzzles of our ambiguous world, and discover the hope-filled possibilities of life.

The story of faith must be constantly retold and interpreted and in that effort the support of the educational life of the community is essential. Yet it is most particularly in the liturgy that this corporate memory lives. All the formative events of the church's heritage are reexperienced in the liturgy—Scripture, sermon, sacrament, and church year. We become participants in the new covenant, not only united with fellow Christians gathered about a particular table but one with all who confess the name of Christ through all times and all places.

The Past Present—Memory. Remembering the past is vital to our self-identity. This is true, whether it be of ourselves as persons, of the Christian community, or of society as a whole. A culture that rejects its memories becomes shallow and tends to lack direction. The past is important, for it is a part of our very being. It has shaped us for what we are, both good and bad. Accepting the past is essential if we are to be able to cope with the uncertainties of the future. Arnold Come has stressed that this "conservation of a sense of history" is a corrective for our contemporary life, illuminating the present:

> The Christian community will keep alive a corporate memory that gives both a sense of continuity to human life and also a sense of direction and hope. As individual man finds meaning only because he holds the whole length and diversity of his life in the unity of memory, so mankind will also find that that people who preserves the racial memory is the source of a sense of meaning for all men.[20]

It becomes important therefore to find ways to affirm our heritage without becoming antiquarian or nostalgic. It is important to free the past so that it can give light to the present. However, we need to take care to avoid an idolizing of the past that holds us back from embracing present and future possibilities. The past must never keep us from hearing God calling us in this present time.

It may be helpful to understand the Jewish concept of memory. To remember was something dynamic, never static. It was a living dimension of present experience.

In instituting the Lord's Supper, Jesus said, "Do this in remembrance of me" (I Cor. 11:24). In order to understand the meaning of these familiar words, we need to remember them in the Jewish way. To remember was to bring the thing remembered out of the past into the present as something effectual and operative. To remember was to make alive, to cause to continue to live.

This understanding of memory lies at the heart of the Passover celebration. Of the institution of the Passover, Scripture states, "This day shall be for you a *memorial* day, and you shall keep it as a feast to the Lord; throughout your generations you shall observe it as an ordinance for ever" (Ex. 12:14, italics added).

The Passover is a sacramental meal. The food is symbolic of the exodus event. Bitter herbs are eaten, because the bondage of Egypt was hard and bitter. Unleavened bread is eaten because the departure from Egypt was made in haste, before the dough could rise. A mixture of fruit and wine symbolizes the Egyptian mud of which the bricks were made. The shank bone is symbolic of the lambs whose blood was placed upon the doorways of the houses of the Israelites to identify and protect the people whom God called. The events of the deliverance which formed the people of God are thus relived sacramentally.

This "memorial" is more than remembering a past event. In the Passover meal, participants in the meal become a part of the Passover event itself. They relive the exodus, which thereby gives meaning and identity to present experience. The past becomes a part of the present moment. They are not spectators of a past event, but sacramentally participants, called to be the people of the covenant just as the ancients were called. The past event of the exodus and present experience thus merge in the paschal meal.

From its inception the Eucharist was celebrated with this Jewish liturgical understanding. Jesus gave his disciples more than something to help them remember when otherwise they might forget. The translation of I Cor. 11:24 as "Do this in remembrance of me" fails fully to convey this Jewish liturgical understanding. It has within it something of the sense of "In doing this, I am present with you."

The Eucharist, like the Passover, brings the mighty act of God in Jesus Christ out of the past and into the present. In eating the bread and drinking the wine, we are at the Lord's Table. We become participants in the cup of the new covenant. We enter into that covenant, and make it our own. We are not spectators of a distant event, but participants, sacramentally, in those past events which give us our identity as the people of God. In the Eucharist, past and present are thus merged.

The Future Present—Hope. The Eucharist not only signifies what God has done but also signifies the possibilities of what is yet to be. The hope of the future and God's activity in the past become "effectually present."

This hope finds expression in the Lord's Supper, for it is an anticipation of the great messianic banquet of the new age, when they "will come from east and west, and from north and south, and sit at table in the kingdom of God" (Luke 13:29). With Christ we eat the bread and drink the wine of his kingdom. Here in this old order we taste "the powers of the age to come" (Heb. 6:5), "the first fruits of the Spirit" (Rom. 8:23). We participate in the life of the new creation, the new age, even here in this present time. We share now a kind of preliminary participation in the kingdom of God that is not yet, that is embodied in Christian hope. Even now, in a world that knows so little righteousness, we celebrate that hope which is the kingdom of God—peace, justice, unity, and love.

The Eucharist is therefore not world-renouncing. In celebrating the sacrament we admit the brokenness of the human situation, and affirm the continuing, living presence of God, who urges this world toward the new creation, the new age. We believe in spite of everything. The result is that both the world and time are given a new sense of worth.

In worship the future should sprout and bud as living hope, giving promise of the possibilities of a new world. Marianne Micks writes that "tomorrow's world is what Christian worship is about."[21] To celebrate the kingdom of God is thus to be open to God's working to make all things new, even to summoning into the present that future which God wills. Such worship is truly creative. This world and time are thus given a new sense of worth.

To embrace both God's past and future within the present gives an expansiveness to liturgy. We relive God's faithfulness in the past, and become confident of God's faithfulness in the future. While liturgy recalls the past, it opens us up to the future, so that we reach out to know even now something of the not yet. We are given direction in our service for God. The interwovenness of past, present, and future is an important dimension to the sacrament. Theologian Norman Pittenger states it succinctly:

> The identity of the Eucharist is established by memory, relationship, and future aim. The "continual remembrance" of the *past,* the *present* communion in the Lord's "presentness" with the mission to be carried out, and the *future* coming of the kingdom already enjoyed in anticipation: here is eucharistic identity.[22]

Thus in merging the past and the future into the present, the Eucharist shares in the ongoing activity of God in the midst of creation. In the dialectic of memory and hope, the people of God are freed to co-create with God in shaping the future.

> His death, O God, we proclaim.
> His resurrection we declare.
> His coming we await.
>   Glory be to you, O Lord.[23]

7. THE MISSIONAL NATURE OF THE SACRAMENT

The Eucharist celebrates the hope of humanity to be found in Jesus Christ. The sacrament should therefore lead us to participate in God's mission and activity in the world. Many of the concepts that have been elaborated above underscore the church's participation in God's mission (e.g., the body of Christ, the messianic feast, the new covenant, the new creation, the kingdom of God, the priesthood of all believers). These have pointed to missional dimensions of both the church and its worship.

When God's purpose for humanity is taken seriously, the church sees itself as a means rather than an end in itself. Engaged in God's mission, the church is taken up into God's work and design for the world. The church exists for the sake of God in the world, as the salt of the earth, the light of the world. Worship and all other aspects of the gathered life of the congregation are first only in order of time. It is God's mission in the world that is ultimate and primary. The church participates in that mission. The main characteristic of the church is thus to be its concern for the world.

The church is to take a leading role in humanizing the world, to be in the vanguard of caring about humanity. It is to demonstrate what it means to be citizens of the kingdom, what it means to be the new creation, the new humanity discovered in Christ.

J. G. Davies, of the University of Birmingham, England, reminds us that it is God's mission, not the church's mission, in which we are to be engaged. It is God's mission that constitutes the very essence of the church. More than simply an aspect of the church's life, this mission touches on the very nature of God himself and his redemptive love for the world. The church is really the church when it is engaged in God's mission and is thus world-centered. Davies points out that this "mission involves peace, integrity, harmony, justice, community—these must be proclaimed *(kērygma);* they must be lived *(koinōnia);* they must be demonstrated *(diakonia).* In mission these three are integrated."[24] The three-fold nature of the mission given the church is to *say,* to *be,* to *do.*

The church needs to understand that it is itself in and of the world, and it must identify with the needs of the world. If the church is faithful to God's mission, the "sanctuary" must not be a flight from the world—a haven of refuge, an escape, or comfortable retreat from worldly involvements. The object of God's love is the whole of humankind; it is not restricted to "church people." Therefore when the church turns in upon itself, unconcerned for the world, it fails its God-given mission, for the very material out of which God will make the new humanity is in the world.

This focus on God's worldly involvement must not be lost in the face of pietistic pressures. The focus of Christianity is more than a concern for souls, even though that too is included. The focus of Christianity is a concern for the whole world. The goal of Christian living is more than making persons whole, even though that too is included. The goal of Christian living is making all of our living together whole— a new heaven and a new earth. The distortions of an excessive individualism place undue attention upon private experience at the expense of public responsibility. Christian energies and resources are too often diverted. Confusion ensues as to the nature of the gospel, the church, and the Christian task in the world. Social problems are largely left to solve themselves in pietism's assumption that society will be reconciled by saving individuals. The full scope of God's love for his world is thereby missed.

Even though the kingdom of God is not yet, we know it already in the church as the firstfruits of the kingdom. We live in the tension between what is and what, in Christian hope, is not yet. And in that tension we engage in God's mission, to the end that the world "can more and more approximate, in more and more places, and more and more times, in more and more ways, and for more and more people, the reign of love and righteousness that is before it as God's plan for his creation."[25]

The true meaning of liturgy is aborted whenever the liturgy becomes for us an escape from responsibility as citizens of the kingdom of God.

For the church engaged in mission, the Eucharist, John A. T. Robinson reminds us, "is the crucible of the new creation, in which God's new world is continually being fashioned out of the old as ordinary men and women are renewed and sent out as the carriers of Christ's risen life."[26]

The fullness of the Christian life is expressed when the church's worship and its God-given mission are united. Worship and mission need each other. When worship and mission are separated, distortions are inevitable. Worship and mission are interdependent. Worship needs mission lest it become esoteric and merely aesthetic. But without worship mission becomes aimless, loses its perspective, and tends toward self-glorification and self-aggrandizement. Worship reminds mission of its source, and mission enables worship to be authentic, related to life.

Worship is therefore the indispensable and life-giving center of all that the church does both in its life together and dispersed in the life of the world. If the church's worship ceases, the community dies, for by its worship the church lives. Worship is the beat of its heart. Like the systole and the diastole of the heart, so worship is for the church a pump that sends into circulation and draws in again. From this life-giving center of Word and sacrament the church spreads abroad into the world to mingle like leaven in the dough, to give seasoning like salt, to illumine like light. Then once more the church returns from the world to its worship, like a fisherman gathering up his nets, or a farmer coming in from the fields having harvested his grain.[27]

The liturgical responsibility of the community therefore does not end with the benediction. The community is charged to continue the liturgy in the life of the world:

> Go into the world in peace; have courage; hold on to what is good; return no one evil for evil; strengthen the fainthearted; support the weak; help the suffering; honor everyone, love and serve the Lord, rejoicing in the power of the Holy Spirit.[28]

Chapter IV

The Use
of Art Forms
in Worship

Like language, art is integral to the liturgy. From the very beginning of civilization, art has been used in the service of worship. Dance, story, painting, sculpture, drama, have all been used in ritual for thousands of years.

The arts are important to worship, for they involve the whole person, elicit all the senses, and provide a fresh way to look at things. The arts help overcome the limitations of worship that is predominantly verbal, for art speaks in a language that is inaccessible to the reasoning mind. The arts express what words alone cannot. Color, sensory experience, fragrance, taste, form, balance, harmony, movement, touch, cannot be adequately explained or described. Our words need that which art can communicate. Architect Edward A. Sovik states that the arts

> penetrate our consciousness and can carry a message with a succinctness, immediacy, subtlety, force, and memorability that words can never muster. This is . . . the virtue of poetry over prose, song over speech, the dances over mere movement, and drama over narrative.[29]

Howard Moody, pastor of Judson Memorial Church in New York City, and an early pioneer in celebrative liturgical forms, states it forcefully: "Without the arts the Church has no language adequate for the communication of her essential realities."[30] He sees the arts as capable of giving greater meaning to our wordy forms of worship:

> I am convinced that we who are conditioned by and captive of a word-drenched worship need desperately to recover the power of the visual arts with their potent impact on the subconscious and unconscious of our psyches. Dance, painting, graphics, and films are non-verbal but basic communicators of our time.[31]

The congregation that Moody serves utilizes the extensive range of artistic talent of the art colony in which the church is located. Evaluating their use of the arts, he writes that they

> enrich ritual acts beyond our hopes and relieved us of the fear that if we did not talk about God, He would disappear. They taught us that if we *sang* of His joy, *danced* in His praise, *bathed* our eyes in the beauty of His creations, that was also worship.[32]

The role of art in liturgy is succinctly stated by Lutheran liturgiologist Luther D. Reed: "Doctrine gives corporate worship a body; history gives it continuity; art gives it wings to soar in the heights."[33]

Religion and art have close links. Each probes the meaning of life. Each describes the human situation. To ignore the arts is to ignore that which perhaps most adequately communicates a depth understanding of the age in which we live and serve. Sculptor and editor Trevor Wyatt Moore reminds us that any art is really religious art whenever it "carries its humanizing symbols to the world," when it is "a mirror of our condition—an aesthetic examination of conscience."[34] When this role of art is recognized, it becomes clear that art in the service of liturgy is not necessarily "religious" art as we have usually understood it. The divisions that have heretofore separated "religious" art from "secular" art ought not apply. Any art that gives a true and deeper insight into the meaning or nature of human existence is appropriate for Christian liturgy.

Moore calls for "a new sense of 'Christian' art that is *not* diverted from the mainstream of life; *not* sorted in 'religious' and 'secular' packets," an art that brings "into Christian experience all expressions of the creative act."[35] When we are able to recognize the "sacred" depths in the heart of the "secular," we will have begun to take seriously the church's doctrine of the incarnation, that God speaks in the depths of life, rather than from outside human existence. Art, in this sense, can be revelatory of the Word in a timely way, whenever the artist is sensitive to life's meaning and experience. In this manner the artist articulates the Christian witness.

It needs to be stressed that art used in the liturgy is to *serve* the liturgy. It is to be subordinate to the action that takes place. It cannot be an end in itself; it cannot threaten, or overpower the action of the liturgy. It is the liturgy itself that is the true art, and whatever art forms are used are used to enhance. Even stylistic church architecture, or appointments, can overpower the liturgical action. A common failure of mod worship is that the media often take over and dominate. But when they serve the liturgy well, the arts can speak eloquently and effectively.

It is important to understand that liturgical art is communal. It is to express the faith of the Christian community, and assist the people in their worship.

It is likewise important that the art that is used be of the best quality that the congregation is capable of creating or understanding. Much art used in the church lacks artistic merit and is therefore inadequate in expressing the praise of God, or proclaiming a revealing Word. Art that is used should be first of all good art. Good art speaks more clearly than poor art. The judgment as to what is good art is highly subjective; nevertheless, good art certainly utilizes good form and style, and is a significant interpretation of some aspects of reality. Daniel Berrigan has said, "Bad art has a way of becoming bad theology, and bad theology in turn cripples life."[36] Whatever art forms are used—dance, drama, literature, textiles, music, architecture—should meet the particular standard of excellence that is demanded by the particular field it represents. It has been suggested that perhaps more artists have been turned away from religious rites by the rites themselves than by the theology they convey.

1. DANCE

Dance is unquestionably the oldest form of art. From the beginning of civilization it has been important to every culture. Gerardus van der Leeuw, in his book *Sacred and Profane Beauty: The Holy in Art,* expresses it in these words:

> The art of beautiful motion is far and away the oldest. Before man learned how to use any instruments at all, he moved the most perfect instrument of all, his body. He did this with such abandon that the cultural history of prehistoric and ancient man is, for the most part, nothing but the history of the dance.[37]

Dance is the most natural expression of the ordered movement of the human body. A composite of spirit and body, dance is a direct outlet for feeling, and is therefore elemental and instinctive as an art form. Transcending words, dance expresses the highest and lowest of human emotions. All other art forms have within them something of this fundamental quality of the art of dance.

It is little wonder that dance originated among primitive people as an indispensable and natural way to express religious faith. In dance, the people sought unity with creation, believing that it was by their dance that the gods were enabled to give all that sustained their lives. It is important to note that these religious dances were highly communal in expression.

Dance in primitive religion may still be observed among the Pueblo Indians of New Mexico. These communal prayer-dances are held at crucial seasonal changes important to the growing and harvesting of crops. Always big occasions, they begin when the first rays of the sun bathe the adobe walls and do not end until the sun sets behind the mountain peaks.

It is typical for the dances to include two groups of dancers, one of men, the other of women. They also include drummers, a chorus, clowns, and masked figures, all choreographed with great precision. The movement and chant are done with exact rhythm and action. The dancers wear elaborate sacred costumes of furs, feathers, pine boughs, and corn-husks. Gourds with pebbles are shaken.

In sound and movement the dancers imitate rain, corn, and wild game. They mimic the sound of seed dropping on the ground, of thunder and rain, the movement of the breeze in pine trees, and the cries of the animals. The male dancers pound the earth with their steps, ordering the seed to live and grow. The women dancers move with soft steps, impassive like the earth, showing how the seed is received and nurtured. The imitative movements and sounds are believed to produce that which is imitated. The corn is thus danced into existence; the rain is danced out of the clouds. These dances express the earliest use of dance as communal prayer.

The Hebrew scriptures are filled with references to dance as the most expressive way to worship God. The joy and freedom of the Jewish faith regularly took the form of dance. For several centuries dance continued in the early church as a part of Christian worship. However, dance was finally all but eliminated, apparently because of the body/soul dualism of Gnosticism. Gnosticism viewed the mind as good, the body (or flesh) as evil. The flesh was to be strictly controlled by the intellect (in which the human person was thought to be most like God). All that remains to remind us that dance

was once a part of Christian worship are some ceremonial
actions and gestures. Van der Leeuw states:

> The dance, once *the* religious art in the strictest sense of the
> word, is today scarcely conceivable as an expression of the holy.
> The Church speaks, sings, paints, and builds, but it does not
> dance; or at least it does so no longer. Once it did dance, . . . and
> occasionally, in some hidden corner, it still does. But its dance
> is a 'relic' and reminds us of the fact that the Christian Church
> is not only a church, but also a superb museum.[38]

Dance, then, is not something new being introduced for
the first time into contemporary worship. It is in fact the
oldest form of worship, and to fail to restore it in some way
is to overlook the basic values that dance can contribute to
worship, and to fail to utilize one of the most basic means of
communication available to us.

Dance in worship restores a feeling of the goodness of the
body. In this way it helps erase the false dichotomy between
body and soul, and restores a sense of the unity and wholeness of being. Van der Leeuw expressed this when he wrote
that in dance "the body moves itself spiritually, the spirit
bodily."[39]

But it is here that dance becomes most controversial. It is
difficult for many to overcome the idea that the body with its
sensuality is evil. We need to overcome the idea that the
sensuousness of dance makes it unfit for worship.

Dance provides a direct form of expressing religious experience. It is much more direct than the reasoned approach.
Sometimes dance alone can say what needs to be said.

There is great value in the formation of a liturgical dance
group from among members of the congregation to assist in
worship, in much the same manner as a choir is used. The
beauty of movement in the service of praise thereby becomes
a part of worship. Help is available to a congregation wanting
to incorporate this valid art form.[40]

Praise in a festival celebration takes on a glorious note when, for example, dance is used along with choral singing, brass and organ, in an arrangement of Psalm 150. Other dances can also be simple, expressing other moods, as for example the dancing of the Magnificat on the Fourth Sunday of Advent. Dance adds much to express the varying moods of the Christian year. It lends itself to Lent quite as well as to Easter and Christmas. It can express the anguish of Good Friday quite as well as the exhilaration of Pentecost.

In the setting of the liturgy, dance is most particularly suited to the use of the psalms. Traditionally, a psalm, capturing the theme of the day, is used between the lesson from the Old Testament and the lessons from the New Testament. In such moments of singing before God, dance seems most fitting. A communal dimension is preserved, while retaining the artful dance of a liturgical dance group, when the dance accompanies the singing of the psalm by cantor or choir, with the congregation singing an antiphon.

Worshipers quite readily identify with the dance interpreters, in much the same way that they are able to identify with a choir. However, some of the same problems that confront a choir are also those of a dance group. Their role is not to entertain but to express the worship of the congregation. There is the ever-present problem of the congregation being in a spectator role.

In order to develop its fullest possibilities, there may be some occasions when dance might involve the congregation. The spectator problem is then fully overcome. Dance that involves an entire group effectively expresses the communality of that group.

There are modest ways in which a congregation that recognizes the value of sacred movement can begin. It is well for most congregations to begin gradually. A congregation might be taught some simple and expressive gestures to accompany the praying of the Lord's Prayer. Simple, unison movement of arms and hands by worshipers conveys that it is *"Our* Father," not *"My* Father." So also, joining hands while saying the creed can express the solidarity of the community of faith.

More use can be made of processionals. The processional originated in dance. Van der Leeuw states that the processional is "a pure and universal relic of the cultic dance." However, it is best viewed, he says, "as a petrified dance, the movement monotonous, no expression of counterpoint. But rhythm is present."[41]

Eucharistic celebration may regularly incorporate a procession in which the gifts of bread, wine, and money are offered at the table. If it is not already the regular practice, the entire congregation might be given the privilege of periodically processing to the table to receive the sacrament while standing about the table. The sacrament thus becomes much more of a communal meal. A communal sense is difficult to attain in pew Communion with persons facing the backs of those seated in front of them. Passion (Palm) Sunday is an appropriate occasion for a worshiping congregation to assemble outside the building for the beginning of worship and at the proper time to process into the worship space while singing, accompanied by brass.

When the congregation as a whole is involved in a procession, a sense of communality is readily conveyed.

2. DRAMA

At the point that dance incorporates pantomime, it begins to become drama. Drama and dance are closely related, for movement is an essential ingredient of drama.

As with dance, drama has a long history of being part of religious observances. In fact, modern theater is the outgrowth of primitive religious ritual. For many centuries the church used drama; the medieval mystery and morality plays are examples.

But more closely related to the liturgy than these plays, which were presented apart from worship, were dramatic interludes during the liturgy itself. Some of these were simple, whereas others were rather elaborate. They might be incorporated at the beginning of the Mass, used in relationship to the reading of the lessons, or appear at the close of worship. They carefully avoided distorting or distracting from the liturgy itself, and sought to involve the people in the underlying rhythm of the celebration. They were most in evidence at Christmas and Eastertide.

Examples include a part of the entrance song, in which some angels and Christians at the tomb engaged in a dialogue that led to the announcement: "He is not here; he is risen as he himself has said. Go and say that he is risen."[42] The Easter Scripture lesson was sometimes followed by the race of Peter and John to the tomb. These brief interludes spoke with directness and intensity, aided by symbolic props and gestures. Daniel A. Kister, in writing about these dramatic interludes in the liturgy, states that they

> must have quickly and forcefully drawn the assembly into an attitude of expectant joy in preparation for an active reception of the word of God. Far from intruding into the liturgical action or dislodging the participating assembly, it sparks a sense of jubilation well suited to the beginning of the Easter celebration.[43]

Kister cites a tenth-century example. In connection with the Good Friday service, a cross wrapped in white linen was buried in a sepulcher. The tomb was then draped with a veil. At the end of Easter morning matins, a monk, representing an angel, with palm branch in hand, was seated at the entrance to the sepulcher. During the third responsory, three others approached the sepulcher. They represented the women who came to the tomb to anoint Jesus' body. The angel asked, "Whom are you seeking?" "Jesus of Nazareth," they answered. "He is not here," the angel announced, "he has risen as he said. Go and spread the news that he has risen from the dead." The three turned to the choir and sang: "Alleluia. The Lord is risen." The angel called them back: "Come and see the place." Then lifting the veil over the sepulcher, the angel showed them that the tomb was empty, void of the cross, and that only the linen in which the cross had been wrapped remained. They laid down the vessels of ointment they had brought with them. They took the linen and held it up to show that the Lord is risen, and sang, "The Lord has risen from the tomb." The linen was then placed on the altar. The head of the assembly rejoiced, and led the congregation in singing the Te Deum Laudamus, while the bells were rung.[44]

This interlude retained the gospel's force. Its actions led directly to the participation of the worshiping congregation in the singing of the Te Deum. Kister emphasizes its liturgical strength when he says, "It belongs to the worshiping assembly, which expresses its joyful faith in Christ's resurrection as the climax of a dramatic experience that is both effective theater and good liturgy."[45]

Interest in the use of drama in worship is reviving today. Chancel drama is being introduced into worship. The plays are usually brief and use no props or at the most a minimal amount of props. They call for some imagination on the part of the viewers. Usually the setting is described to the viewers for them to fill in mentally before the play takes place. Chancel drama can be used as sermons, or as particular portions of worship, such as the call to worship or a part of the confession of sin.

Religious drama has generally been very mediocre. However, this is changing, and help is beginning to be available for churches wanting to introduce drama into worship.[46]

In the use of drama, care needs to be taken lest important

aspects of worship be removed from the people and they become even more spectators of something being done for them. Nevertheless, properly used, chancel drama can convey a message with clarity and eloquence. Drama is an art form that ought not to be overlooked in ways that will enhance the liturgy.

3. LITERATURE

Literature was the principal art form of the Hebrew people, their artistic creativity being concentrated chiefly in writing. The result is that much of the Old Testament is great by any literary standards.

The artistic use of words has been the strength of the liturgy throughout the centuries, and is an example of good art. Worship has generally excelled in the effective use of words, though at times the directness and the force of the liturgy have been lost in its beauty and cadence.

The liturgy ought to possess artistic sensitivity while having force and directness that communicate. Words are essential to communication, even though we have too exclusively used the verbal. Those who lead worship need to be good craftspersons in the use of words.

We might note that writings from other sources than Scripture often can be used in the liturgy. Some can be used to amplify or bring out a particular contemporary meaning of a Scripture lesson. Some brief readings lend themselves well for use in relationship to confession, intercession, call to worship, benediction, etc.

One example of the use of contemporary readings is the service on the First Sunday of Advent 1974 at the church of which I was then pastor. The fall of 1974 was a particularly discouraging period in national life. People became callous because of bad news that had come in big doses and they tended to be shockproof. A sense of defeatism prevailed. The

Advent message of hope seemed to have a sense of urgency about it. Immediately before the confession of sin, an editorial that had appeared in the local newspaper a few days earlier was read. The editorial deplored the defeatism and callousness, "the prevailing sentiment that nothing can or will be done to change the negative direction of events, and, worse still, the lessening of popular demand that something be done." After documenting numerous evidences of the loss of hope, it stated, "For when a nation loses hope, it is time for the eulogy to be written."[47] The prayer of confession followed, confessing our prevailing despair and loss of hope:

> We confess that we do not expect your kingdom. We are calloused and defeated in the face of crisis. We have lost hope that anything can or will be done to bring about change. . . . Rekindle hope within us that we may once more eagerly and expectantly seek the fulfillment of your kingdom. Amen.[48]

The day's lectionary readings reflected the hope implicit in the Scripture:

> Nations . . . shall beat their swords into plowshares,
>   and their spears into pruning hooks;
> nation shall not lift up sword against nation,
>   neither shall they learn war any more.
>
> (Isa. 2:4)

> Remember how critical the moment is. It is time for you to wake out of sleep. . . . It is far on in the night; day is near. Let us therefore throw off the deeds of darkness and put on our armour as soldiers of the light. (Rom. 13:11–12, NEB)

A contemporary reading followed the Scriptures. It was chosen from the writings of Erich Fromm, in which the need for hope is effectively underscored:

> To hope means to be ready at every moment for that which is not yet born, and yet not become desperate if there is no birth in our lifetime. There is no sense in hoping for that which already

exists or for that which cannot be. Those whose hope is weak settle down for comfort or for violence; those whose hope is strong see and cherish all signs of new life and are ready every moment to help the birth of that which is ready to be born.[49]

When hope has gone life has ended, actually or potentially. Hope is an intrinsic element of the structure of life, of the dynamic of man's spirit.[50]

The sermon emphasized that Advent renews for us the vision of the kingdom of God. Advent helps us understand the importance of hope, relates us to the source of hope which is in God, and rekindles hope in our lives. Advent thereby challenges us to an active involvement as agents of the kingdom's coming.

The use of contemporary materials, particularly because they were from secular sources, well written and timely, gave a note of relevance to the day's theme and the emphasis of the Advent season.

4. MUSIC

Throughout the centuries the value of the art of music in worship has been recognized. Music has long been the principal means of congregational praise and thanksgiving. It has spared worship from being completely dry and arid verbiage.

Unfortunately for the past three or four hundred years, the church has lived by a sharp distinction between sacred and secular styles of music. The idea persists that there is a distinctly "church style" of music that is to determine what is or is not proper in worship. However, when we understand that the Christian experience encompasses all human experience, we realize that the distinctions between secular and sacred are largely false. The tragic result of this dichotomy is that it produces the feeling that the church is really not a part of the world in which we live, for the music of the church speaks of a different world from that which we daily experience.

The old rules determining what style of music is appropriate for the church are not valid anymore. We cannot continue to defend a limited range of musical style as the only style appropriate for worship. We cannot make a clear distinction between church music and secular music, just as we cannot make a clear distinction between Christian art and non-Christian art.

Musical styles in themselves are neutral. If any distinction can be made between sacred and secular, it would have to be determined by the use to which the style is put rather than the style itself. When given religious content, folk, jazz, and rock can all be used effectively in worship.

Contemporary musical styles can demonstrate the church's belief in incarnation, as the Word becomes enfleshed in the modality of the day. If we truly believe that religious experience pertains to the totality of human experience, then contemporary musical styles can be of immeasurable value in witnessing to the wholeness of the gospel. Contemporary music, speaking the language of our day, is closely related to all aspects of society. Much contemporary music speaks with an honesty that is not always easily discerned in more traditional forms of church music. When contemporary styles are used in the church, they can help the church to become more sensitive to the world in which we live.

There is value in using music that is not self-consciously religious. Folk songs, such as protest songs, have been used effectively in relationship with confession of sin. The world of reality and the world God desires are thus held in juxtaposition. The music of Bob Dylan and of Simon and Garfunkel has found its place in liturgy from time to time. Often some of the music originating outside the church expresses a sense of Christian value with greater clarity than much "church music." Its use in worship is a way of meeting God where he is at work in the culture, a celebration of God's presence in the human world outside church structures.

When the prejudice against newer musical styles is broken down, an exciting breadth of possibility is opened up. Even though it once seemed inconceivable that "secular" music could ever be used to serve liturgy, changes are now taking place in the music of the church and opening up a wide range of exciting possibilities.

The challenge to the persons who shape the music used by the church is perhaps greater than it has been at any other time in history. Consider the variety of styles that can be utilized—jazz, classical, pop, folk, rock, and now electronic. Heinz Werner Zimmermann sees a possibility for a new heterogeneous polyphony, bringing together the great plurality of different musical voices that are available—"a new polyphony," he writes, "which acknowledges the individuality of each voice and yet leads them together into a higher polystylistic wholeness."[51] While expressing the value of the new styles, he stresses the importance of retaining the traditional forms as a part of this heterogeneous polyphony:

> We must first reject the folly of supposing that we can ever achieve again one unified modern style for church music. All that we have musically inherited cannot be thrown into oblivion. We shall continue to live with the great works from the past. The music of the past is in our musical blood. In the church also we shall continue to live the great works of the past. We shall not throw them aside in closed-minded iconoclasm. With all our efforts to create new songs for the church we shall continue to sing the old hymns. With all our efforts to create new music for organ and choir for divine worship we shall continue to hear the works of those masters who have gone before us. We shall creatively carry forward the tradition in our worship and not abolish it.[52]

Variety is most desirable, both in musical styles and in the use of musical instruments, a variety that includes both new and old, sacred and secular, the many musical instruments as well as the organ.

The fundamental criterion for selecting music for worship is that it be *good* music, according to the standards of the particular style it represents. There is both good and bad contemporary music. The question of quality should not be invalidated. Erik Routley, noted English musicologist, has said, "Defect in music, as in the church, is simply what Thomas Aquinas called *privatio boni*—the absence of good where good ought to be."[53] He says, "Bad music is music that to some extent fails to *be*—it has a touch of infantilism or imbecility."[54]

In recent years an astounding number of contemporary religious songs have been published. Few have any genuine conception of contemporary musical style. Consequently much of this music is poor according to the musical standards of the particular style it represents. Most of it is commercial, produced primarily, it appears, to meet a demanding market. Most of it is poor poetry by literary standards. Furthermore, little of it is written with an understanding of the nature of the liturgy or of contemporary theology. Therefore, with so much of it being poor music, poor poetry, and poor theology, a great deal of sorting is necessary. Contemporary music is needed that combines good music, good poetry, and good theology.

Dennis Fitzpatrick, composer, musician, and publisher of many contemporary religious songs, makes the following statements concerning musical criteria:

> The criteria that I would apply to popular music in church are the same that I would apply to a classical music style: first, that it be well composed within the style chosen; second, that it be well performed; third, that it be textually suitable; and last, that it be appropriate music for the actual congregation present.[55]

Roman Catholic composer C. Alexander Peloquin, one of the greatest composers of choral music using contemporary styles, points to hopeful beginnings that correct the deficiencies:

> What is being done today that is important is the creation of a quality repertoire with a totally new outlook on the liturgy: a new psychology, a new theology, that will not go without its Karl Rahner, Teilhard de Chardin, its Kung, or its John XXIII.[56]

A church's music program can involve all age groups, utilizing a variety of contemporary musical styles along with the traditional. Antiphonal music (between choir and congregation) is an enjoyable experience and enables a congregation to be involved with the more complex singing of a choir, while conveying a sense of belonging. The psalms of Joseph Gelineau are widely used in both Roman Catholic and Protestant churches. These feature a soloist or choir singing the text of the psalms, with the congregation singing an easily learned antiphon as a response at appropriate intervals. Many musical instruments ought to be used as well as the organ, for example, recorders, flutes, violins, viola, drums, guitar, and bassoon.[57]

Music is important to the liturgy and can greatly help enrich the use of the senses and the total involvement of life in worship. John Killinger, in recognizing this value of music, points out how it is needed to balance the more mental aspects of worship:

> Religion is sung, whistled, stamped, danced, clapped, more than it is *thought*. There should exist a precarious balance between the two, of course; but it is essential that thought not prevail always over the ability to vent the emotions rhythmically. When it does the sense of God becomes dry, brittle, chimerical, not because he is dry and brittle but because we are.[58]

5. TEXTILES

There is currently a renewed interest in the creative use of textile art in worship. Creatively designed paraments, banners, wall hangings, and vestments are more and more finding their rightful place.

Banners. The emergence of banners as an art form is actually a renewal of medieval art. Well-designed banners or wall hangings can add a colorful and celebrative note to worship. They have movement, catching any air current, and they stimulate the sense of touch. They need not be elaborate. Changed frequently, they can add a useful variety and with ease can change the tone of the setting of worship. In a sense the whole interior decoration of a space can be modified by the use of banners. One value is that they are not permanent and can be disposed of when no longer desired.

Care should be taken to assure that they are well designed. The best tend to be abstract and symbolic. Words ought not be used unless they are symbolic words, such as *shalom, peace, joy, alleluia, hosanna.* Care ought to be taken that the symbols used carry contemporary meaning. Some of the traditional symbols have little value today because the meanings they convey no longer live.

Outdoor banners might also be explored. A large outdoor banner, such as a long streamer from a high tower, may be a beautiful and effective witness to the joy of the gospel.

A major value of banners is in their ability to engage the creativity of the congregation. Banners appropriate for the particular church community may be developed.

Paraments. Textiles are also used in relationship to pulpit and table. Paraments ordinarily are coordinated thematically with the Christian year, and also can add much color to worship. Like banners, they can be made by members of the congregation. Inexpensive, simply made sets can mean a larger selection, and result in more frequent changes used to convey symbolically the changing themes of the days and seasons.

Vestments. Another use of textile art that is finding creative expression is vestments. Acceptance of interesting vestments is widening to include churches that traditionally have given them little or no attention. Even those Protestant churches which traditionally use only black pulpit gowns are changing. Colorful stoles, white robes, even traditional eucharistic vestments such as the alb and the chasuble are beginning to appear in heretofore unlikely places. It seems appropriate for colorful vestments to replace the black robes especially in the celebration of the eucharistic festival.

The design possibilities of the chasuble are greater than for any other liturgical vestment. Deriving from daily dress in early Roman society, the chasuble has endured as the classic eucharistic vestment. The chasuble covers the entire body like a loose-fitting, oversized poncho. It is simply made. Once a design is developed, it can easily be made by someone in the congregation who is skilled in the art of sewing.

Custom-made vestments, possessing greater artistry than their catalog versions, are also available. It should be borne in mind that simplicity is more in keeping with modern taste than richly crafted vestments.

It is appropriate on occasion to provide all the worshipers with some kind of vestment. For example, on the Sunday following Easter parishioners might be given white stoles of paper, signifying the newness of the Easter season. The stoles would be worn throughout the service. The removal of the stoles after worship would symbolize the rolling up of the sleeves for the renewing of Christ's work in the world.

Marion P. Ireland, an artist who has done extensive work with textiles, has expressed the positive contribution that well-designed textile art can give to worship when she says that vestments and paraments "may be a joyful thing—a celebration, an act of praise, an offering on behalf of the artist and the congregation. It may be a testimony to God, an affirmation of faith, and an alleluia."[59]

6. CERAMIC ART AND SCULPTURE

Attention ought to be given to the vessels used in the sacrament. Often persons skillful in ceramics or metalwork can fashion a chalice and flagon appropriate to the region, with greater contemporary artistic beauty than the traditional silver pieces that are ordered from catalogs.

Variety may be introduced by using a different cross for each season of the Christian year, to be hung over the holy table, or mounted on the wall behind the table. An appropriate cross for Lent would be the tau cross; for Good Friday, the crucifix; for Advent, the Christus Rex; for Christmas, Easter, and Pentecost, a richly ornamented cross; for Epiphany, the Epiphany cross. This would be one more way to mark the seasons.

7. FLOWERS AND PLANTS

The skilled use of flowers and native plants of the region can support the thematic focus of the liturgy. Floral offerings of the people and of the countryside can be used both in narthex displays and in the worship space itself. For example, grapes and stocks of dried wheat may be used to suggest the Christian sacramental relationship of Passover and the Eucharist, when the Paschal Supper is eaten. In the Southwest, yuccas can be used in addition to palms for Passion (Palm) Sunday. Bonelike cacti and succulents may be used in ways that support Lenten themes. Flame-colored gladioli may symbolize the flames of Pentecost; the tri-petaled iris may be used for Trinity Sunday. This suggests the potential of floral arrangements to enhance the thematic focus of the day or the season.

8. PHOTOGRAPHY

A truly modern artistic medium is photography. Photography makes available the entire range of visual arts. Great classic paintings, primitive art, landscape, contemporary art, pictures of people and events, can all be utilized in effective ways.

Projected images teach, inspire, and enhance worship, and are invaluable in celebrating the Christian year. A picture can quickly convey meanings, or applications of the theme, much more effectively than words alone. Dependence upon hymnals and orders of service can be reduced by using slides. Slides of the hymns (white on black) can be projected, superimposed with illustrative slides. Words of creeds, prayers, and responses can be projected at the moment the congregation is to participate, thereby relieving some of the tension of unfamiliarity with an order of service or of trying to find the right place in the service book or the order of worship. Permission to photograph copyrighted words or music can be requested from the music publishers.

In the building or remodeling of liturgical space a simple projection room might be provided. A projection room eliminates mechanical and intrusive aspects such as visibility of equipment, projector noise, and the busyness of operators. If a projection room is not possible, an attractive enclosure for projectors can be mounted on the ceiling or a wall, with the operator unobtrusively using a remote-control device.

The church that has large wall space painted white is fortunate in that a screen becomes unnecessary. Projection screens are not visually attractive and are awkward to use. When the screens are not in use for other portions of worship, their presence is an intrusion on the worshiping community.

The screen suggests something tacked on, instead of its becoming an integral part of worship. If a white wall seems overly stark when not used for projections, banners or other movable art might break the monotony of the space. However, if designed well, such a wall can be attractive and blend well in the total environment.

With the use of multiple projectors interesting effects are possible, such as the superimposing and fading of images. The development of a slide library can provide material for use even on those occasions when insufficient time is available for much advanced planning.

In the use of projections, care must be taken not to detract from the important actions of the liturgy itself. The use of slides can result in impressing people with a fine "show" rather than in enhancing the act of worship. As with all the arts, the role of projections is a supportive role, the liturgical action itself being in the starring role. Because photography is a very strong medium, great care must be taken in its use, lest it take over and dominate all else that is done. Projections, therefore, should ordinarily not be used during the reading of the lessons, the presentation of the sacramental elements, the eucharistic prayer, the words of institution, or while the people are receiving the sacrament. Slides can often be selected to enhance these major liturgical acts, but they are best used immediately following the action itself, thereby reinforcing meanings rather than competing with the liturgical action. Nothing should ever compete with or detract from the drama of the liturgical acts themselves. The liturgy is the principal art; all other arts are supportive.

Projections need to be used with great discrimination, selectivity, and taste. The common fault in their use is overuse. It is better to use them with a light touch rather than saturate a congregation with projections. But when properly used, projected images give the liturgy a contemporaneity, a beauty, and an immediate application available in no other medium. The contribution that photography can make to worship is well worth learning the techniques of using it.

9. LIGHT

An often overlooked medium is light. Light can be used artistically in subtle and skillful ways. It can make an innovative contribution to worship in some liturgical spaces. In addition to the use of seasonal colors for paraments and vestments, colored light appropriate to the day or the season can be used. For example, one church on the First Sunday of Advent illumined the wall behind the table with a softly glowing rose-tinted purple light. The parishioners upon entering the space were immediately reminded that it was the season of Advent.

One problem that must be dealt with in the design of liturgical space is the need to maintain a balance between the otherness of God and the communality of the people. Numerous ways have been attempted to convey this balance, especially by creating a tension between horizontal and vertical lines. Light can also be effective in achieving this balance. Brightly illumining the liturgical activity at pulpit, holy table, or font while the remainder of the space has soft light can give an atmosphere of expectancy. This can be done without being theatrical. Theatrics convey an atmosphere of unreality, but the judicious use of light can focus attention upon the liturgical act and give it magnitude.

10. LITURGICAL ARCHITECTURE

Liturgical architecture is another important aspect of the use of art in worship. Every congregation that builds even the simplest structure to house its worshipers is involved in one form of art, whether it is good or bad. Worship space deserves the most careful planning.

The best liturgical architecture results when building committees give careful consideration to the meaning of worship, and design the building for liturgical activity. Buildings are to be designed according to what happens inside of them—designed from the inside out. This is in harmony with modern architecture which works from the basic premise that "form follows function."

When shaped by theology and liturgy, the building will not be merely the setting of the liturgy but will become a part of the liturgy itself, speaking to the worshiper, expressing something of the nature of the church, Christian faith, and worship. Our buildings either make it easier to understand the meaning of what we are doing in worship or they fight against it, and make understanding difficult. It is therefore important to so shape the building for worship that when it is used it will shape us in accordance with the best insights of our faith.

In the expression of the communal understanding of Christian worship the position of the liturgical centers (pulpit, font, and table) is important. The location of the baptismal font suggests that baptism is either a private act or an act incorporating a person into the body of Christ. The holy table by its design emphasizes either the individualistic sacrificial aspect of the sacrament or the meal aspect of the sacrament which clearly conveys the communal dimension. Furthermore, location of the people will suggest either a group of individuals in a spectator role or a community participating in the action. The design possibilities of pulpit, table, and font can also enhance and give meaning to the liturgical actions they facilitate.

A single, unified space, rather than the two-room chancel-nave, seems logically best suited to stress the unity of God's people. The single space further helps eliminate the implication that God is more real in the area screened off from the people, where the clergy conduct worship. God is no more present in one part of the space than in another, but is present in the midst of his people.

It is clear that the long, narrow nave and remote chancel, with the people lined up row upon row in military fashion facing a distant wall, does not contribute to a sense of community or of participation. The semicircular arrangement is more effective in the development of community. However, in our zeal to recover a sense of community we must not lose the sense of the holy. To replace the former otherworldliness with mere sociability would be simply to move from one extreme to another. The church is a community, but a community bound together with its Lord, symbolized in the metaphor of the church as the body of Christ. The best liturgical space symbolizes both of these relationships—God and human, and the human with fellow humans.

Contemporary liturgical architecture should express a true hospitality. This is in keeping with the concept of the church as a family. It should do this without a feeling of clubiness or living room coziness which tends to domesticate God.

Contemporary liturgical architecture will also express simplicity. Superfluous elements will be eliminated. The focus will clearly be upon essentials. Churches are so often cluttered with nonessentials that the primary things are not readily recognized. Font, holy table, and pulpit need to be clearly recognized as the centers of liturgical action.

Contemporary liturgical architecture also demands a flexibility unknown in the past. The space for worship should accommodate different kinds of services in varying circumstances and for different occasions. There will no doubt be more varied types of worship in the future. In providing space for worship, churches need to anticipate such developments and make certain that the space for worship will accommodate the needs of the future. Greater flexibility is achieved if nothing is nailed down. Movable seating that is attractive, comfortable, versatile, and stackable is now available. This permits varying configurations of seating. Churches are now being built with movable liturgical centers (pulpit, table, font). In this way it is possible to have a "different church" for different kinds of celebration, and to arrange the worship space in the most appropriate manner for the occasion. There is value in remodeling existing churches to accommodate the greatest degree of flexibility that may be possible.

The rich benefits to be gained in using all the arts in worship are manifold. The arts express what words alone cannot. They deepen our sense of awe. They attune our whole being to praise. They share the boundless beauty of God which they attempt to express.

"For glory and for beauty," through every artistic means, let all that is beautiful help the people to glorify God.

Chapter V

Creative Possibilities in Liturgical Practice

Flexibility, innovation, and variety are needed elements in the planning and leading of Christian worship. Creative imagination and sensitivity are therefore called for in order that worship might communicate the magnitude of its content as adequately as possible. Just as life itself is spiced with variety, and routine needs to be broken up, liturgical celebration is enhanced by variety, thereby avoiding the monotonous dreariness of so much liturgical practice. Worship should move like a lively conversation, avoiding all false solemnity. Without losing a sense of familiarity with worship, liturgy ought to be varied and fresh.

1. PLANNING FOR WORSHIP

The planning of worship is most effective when it is the responsibility of more than just the minister(s), and involves an active and sensitive committee. Such a committee should include all who share any aspect of the leadership of worship —ministerial, professional, and lay. Persons skilled in various art forms are valuable participants in such a committee. An effective means of adult education is to include other members of the congregation in the planning of worship.

Although it may seem cumbersome and slow to involve

such a group in planning worship (compared with the pastor doing the work alone), it contributes, as nothing else does, to an understanding that worship is the action of a community. Furthermore, it helps to make the liturgy appropriate to the particular congregation, for through inclusion of other members of the congregation in addition to those directly responsible for leading worship, opportunity is given to express the questions, concerns, and feelings of the people.

Fundamental to such a committee is the study of the nature and meaning of worship. The committee also needs a clear sense of appropriate liturgical norms. The committee should carefully plan how each season or festival will be observed. It will arrange for particular groups to plan the various aspects of the worship. It will train ushers and readers, and it will guide occasional musicians. It will continuously examine the congregation's worship pattern, encourage fresh ideas, and always seek ways to bring about liturgical renewal.

Prior to each planning meeting, committee members need to familiarize themselves with the Scripture readings for the day or days under consideration. In cooperation with the minister, the group together will then focus upon the theme that is most appropriate, and determine the manner in which that theme can be developed, using a variety of methods, forms, and artistic expressions. Church bulletins are now available that have cover designs illustrating some theme of the lectionary readings.

All of this will be done, not in isolation of such burning issues as hunger and poverty, concerns for peace and human rights, but in recognition of the fact that worship is fundamental to mission. Such concerns will ever find expression in liturgical planning.

2. Ceremonial Acts and the Leading of Worship

Careful consideration needs to be given to the ceremonial used in worship. Ceremonial refers, not to the text of a liturgical rite, but rather to the way worship is done, to actions in performing the liturgy which seek to make the meaning of the gospel more intelligible. The conscious use of ceremonial furthermore recognizes that the worship of God properly involves the body as well as the mind.

Protestants are generally suspicious of such ceremonial acts as the sign of the cross, genuflecting, and gospel procession. Nevertheless ceremonial is always present in every style of worship, even though it may not be recognized as such. Furthermore, there is worthwhile ceremonial and there is ceremonial that serves little or no purpose. Frequently the utilitarian acts associated with worship are unduly formal and exaggerated—for example, candles lit with grave solemnity, the ushering and taking of the offering like soldiers on parade, choir processionals every Sunday. Stiff formality should be avoided in reference to such functions and not given needless ceremonial, thereby leaving ceremonial possibilities to the liturgy itself.

Simple ceremonial movement can aid communication. For example, there is value in leading each of the various acts of worship from the portion of the worship space that is appropriate to the particular action rather than leading the entire service from one spot. Such movement can communicate something of the meaning of the liturgical act itself. Too often everything, except the sacraments, is led from the pulpit. The pulpit is best reserved for the readings and the sermon. Other places are more appropriate for other actions. It was the practice of the Reformers to perform all portions of the liturgy from the holy table with the exception of the lessons and the sermon. The opening portion of worship, including the confession, may be led either from a position behind the table or from the midst of the people. Intercession, when led from the midst of the people, helps convey the sense of the communality of the prayers. Baptisms might be administered from a place at the entrance to the seating area nearest the main entry into the building, thus signifying entry into the Christian community. By thus dispersing the liturgical actions, movement and space contribute to their meaning.

An alternative to providing extra sheets of paper containing words of songs or prayers is to photograph the portions of the liturgy that are used by the people and project them at the proper time. This improves their involvement in the celebration by utilizing the visual more effectively, and should help reduce any self-consciousness that may be present. It frees the people from having loose papers in their hands and having to follow the entire liturgy of the day, word by word. They can listen to those portions led by others, without being confined to a printed page for everything. Worship should be more than reading, it is seeing the actions of the liturgy as well. When people's faces are buried in a book or when they have to shuffle cumbersome participation materials, they tend to miss the communicative value of visual movement. Their attention is drawn away from the action of the community, and thus they have less sense of being in dialogue. Therefore, there is value in providing the people with only those portions of the liturgical text which involve them, and those are most effective when projected.

The leader of worship ought to consider how his or her hands are used in worship. Gestures ought to be appropriate to the liturgical text. For example, in extending a greeting, such as "Lift up your hearts," the hands of the leader of worship are opened and the arms are widely extended toward the people. With the words, "Let us give thanks to the Lord our God," the hands are rejoined. Hands ought to be as free as possible of books, bulletins, and papers at all times during worship to enable appropriate gestures to be made. The leader of worship should avoid carrying books and papers in moving from one liturgical center to another. To facilitate this, there needs to be adequate advanced planning and placement of liturgical texts at appropriate liturgical centers.

No ceremonial act should draw undue attention to itself; rather, it should be an instrument to point to the presence of God. Any ceremonial act that is introduced and is not familiar to the people needs an accompanying instruction as to its meaning, for worship is an expression of the people, not just the minister.

Silence can be an effective part of the liturgy, expressing the communality of the people. Silence is appropriate after confession, during a bidding prayer, or after all have communed. When it follows the readings from Scripture, or the sermon, it provides opportunity for worshipers to meditate on what they have heard.

The communal dimension of worship increasingly becomes clear when a congregation is encouraged to use the corporate "Amen" after prayers which the worship leader has offered. This affirms that the prayers are theirs and that the worshipers are unified with the leader in the petitions.

Care needs to be taken to guard against redundancy in the leadership of worship. Examples include announcing page numbers and hymns when included in a worship folder, making unnecessary announcements, adding flourishes after the reading of Scripture such as "May the Lord add his blessing to the reading of his precious Word" (as if anything could be added that is not already present).

When members of the congregation are involved with ministers in leading worship, clerical domination of worship is minimized and the communal nature of worship is given vivid expression.

3. Using Liturgies

There is great value in retaining the traditional order of worship and the various elements embodied in it when ordering contemporary worship. The traditional liturgical structure may be outlined as follows:

a. Gathering together in the Lord's name (which may include confession).
b. Readings from Old and New Testaments.
c. Proclamation and response to the Word of God.
d. Prayers of the people for church and world.
e. The peace.
f. Preparation of the table (offertory).
g. Thanksgiving.
h. Breaking of the bread.
i. Eating and drinking together.

This classic order is now embodied in the official or semiofficial liturgical text of nearly every denomination.

The value of retaining this order, even for "creative" celebrations, rests in the fact that it has valued historic roots and has stood the test of time. It contributes a fullness that creative celebrations often lack. Furthermore, it helps to assure a psychologically satisfying experience.

Even though different forms may be used in the order, its use gives worshipers a frame of reference and therefore provides a needed sense of familiarity. The liturgy gets in the way of worship if each week worshipers must be retaught what they may expect. Even though the accepted liturgical text in a particular denomination may be used to greater or lesser degrees (or not at all, depending upon the situation), there is much to be said for retaining the classic order.

This is to suggest that a given liturgy ought to be used with freedom. When unduly confined, worship becomes stilted. But the absence of any familiar norm results in self-consciousness, and the vehicle becomes an end in itself. Liturgies are made for people, not people for a particular liturgy. To use a liturgy without freedom is to misunderstand the intent of liturgy. It is a standard, a norm, a model.

A great deal of variety, innovation, and flexibility is therefore possible within the classic liturgical structure. Some of those possibilities are now suggested. Both traditional and innovative elements are here blended together.

4. THE ENTRANCE RITE

Prelude, or the Preparation. The beginning of worship should remind us that we are a community gathered to worship. There are several ways in which the people may prepare themselves for worship—prayer, silently listening to instrumental music, and meditation.

If unfamiliar hymns or responses are to be used in the liturgy of the day, it may be wise to rehearse them informally. In addition to their learning the new elements of the liturgy, it can relax people and help to eliminate any undue formality that people may be carrying into the gathering. A rehearsal can also provide an opportunity for people to relate to one another and become acquainted with those about them.

Friendly greetings among the members of the community of faith is also an appropriate way for them to prepare for worshiping together. A strong sense of the communal nature of worship suggests that it is inappropriate to become wholly absorbed in private meditation and prayer prior to the liturgy. Greeting one another and conversing together enhances the communal understanding, and can foster an atmosphere of congeniality. In seating visitors, ushers might introduce them to the persons with whom they will be sitting during worship.

It does not seem, however, that both instrumental music and conversation should go on at the same time. The music is not intended to be a cover-up for conversation which becomes louder as the music increases in volume. A carefully chosen and artistically presented instrumental selection is part of the worship and deserves to be listened to by those present. If the instrumental music is not omitted in preference to congenial conviviality, it might be limited to a single selection, with conversation encouraged prior to the music.

Brief concerts have long characterized a prelude to worship. Where used, they can help convey the spirit of the day. Other instruments might be used in addition to, or instead of, the organ. Flute, violin, trombone, timpani, trumpet, or guitar can all be used to contribute to the particular theme of the day or the season. To convey a more austere character, the prelude and the postlude might be omitted during the Lenten season, and a period of silence mark the preparation.

It is preferable that the ministers and those assisting in worship take their places for the leadership of worship by passing through the assembled people rather than through a chancel entrance. This heightens the communal aspect and avoids the appearance of a performer coming on stage.

The choir need not participate in this procession each Sunday, perhaps reserving a choral procession for festival days or seasons. Ordinarily the choir should unobtrusively take its place during the prelude (or prior to the prelude) ready to assist the congregation in its singing.

Upon entering, the ministers may remain in a place with the people instead of going immediately to the holy table or the pulpit. From such a position amid or near the people, they can lead the congregation in the opening rite. This emphasizes the communal nature of the penitential act. However, if the opening rite is not led from a place near or among the people, it ought to be led from behind the holy table.

Call to Worship. In the call to worship the people are reminded that worship centers upon God, and are called to give glory to God. Scripture is spoken which is appropriate to this conviction. It is proper that it refer to the particular liturgical day or season that is being celebrated.

The call to worship is also a greeting. The minister faces the people, and greets them, in recognition of a community worshiping together. This is clearly conveyed when the traditional greeting is used as a part of the call, the pastor saying, "The Lord be with you." The people respond, "And also with you." For variety, the peace might be exchanged at this point in the service rather than later.

It is preferable that the call to worship be spoken from memory. Arms extended naturally toward the people can convey in action what the words signify.

If there is to be a choral procession, the Scriptural call to worship may be spoken from the entrance into the nave. To avoid the awkwardness of greeting the people from behind them, the greeting may be given after the entrance hymn, on such occasions, when the minister has taken his or her place with or before the people.

The Entrance Hymn. The opening hymn should contribute to the deepening of the unity of the people. It may be a psalm or hymn of praise, and it should be chosen with care. It should be familiar to the people; this is no place to have an unfamiliar hymn.

A festive and triumphant character is achieved if at the major festivals—Christmas, Easter, Pentecost (and perhaps the Sundays following Christmas and Easter)—the choir enters with the minister(s) and others who have part in the liturgy during the singing of a processional hymn. Banners announcing the theme of the day's celebration might be carried as a part of such a procession. Brass instruments may be used to provide a descant. The incorporation of musical instruments with the singing at appropriate places in the liturgy helps make the praise of God more glorious, and increases the participation of other members of the congregation.

The Confession of Sin and the Declaration of Pardon. As suggested above, it is appropriate that the confession be led from near or among the people. This clearly unites the leader of worship with the people in expressing their common need of God's forgiving grace. Following the entrance hymn the pastor faces the people and invites them to confession. If standing (or kneeling) near or among the people, the leader of worship, during the prayer, ought to face in the same direction as those with whom he or she is praying. The minister is thus merged with the people in confession. Following a moment of silence, the leader again faces the people and announces the declaration of pardon (preferably from memory). After the sung response, the minister moves to the pulpit (or lectern) for the liturgy of the Word.

If the confession is not led from near or among the people, the minister will lead the people in the penitential rite while standing behind the holy table, facing the people. The pulpit should be avoided as a place to lead the congregation in any portion of the opening rite, reserving it for the liturgy of the Word.

The prayer of confession may have other forms than the usual unison prayers. It can be in the form of a bidding prayer, in which case the petitions should be timely, specific, pertinent, and carefully planned. The petitions might take the form of "We confess . . ." An appropriate response of the people would be, "Forgive us, O Lord." The prayer may be in the form of a litany. Or, the confession may be offered by members of the congregation, either spontaneously or prepared, either in the form of biddings to prayer or brief prayers.

Silent prayer following the corporate prayer gives an opportunity for personal prayer in relationship to the liturgical prayer of the church. Care should be taken to provide ample time. The tendency is always to provide too little time rather than too much. Or, silent prayer may precede rather than follow the confession.

The Kyrie ("Lord have mercy . . ." or "You are the Lord, giver of mercy . . .") is a traditional response to the declaration of pardon. On festival occasions the Gloria in Excelsis ("Glory to God in the highest . . .") is a fitting response. It is rich in tradition and one of the greatest examples of praise that the church possesses. It should be sung with enthusiasm and joy. For festivals, brass instruments, timpani, or cymbals may be used to accompany the first and third paragraphs. The Te Deum or Alleluias are also suitable responses to the declaration of pardon. Of these, only the Kyrie is appropriate to the spirit of Lent and Advent. In addition to these traditional liturgical responses, many hymns are appropriate for use as a response to the declaration of pardon. The singing should always move briskly, and never be somber.

The confession may, on occasion, be relocated within the liturgy. For example, it may follow the creed, in which case the peace might be exchanged after the confession. If a creed is not used, the confession could follow the sermon.

Another variation would be to delay the opening hymn until after the confession is offered, thus emphasizing confession as an act preparatory to worship. Or, perhaps occasionally the people could assemble in the narthex or another room as they arrive for worship, where the confession would be made. Then the people would join in a procession, entering the worship room with joy.

The visual projection of slides or a brief motion picture can occasionally be incorporated into the penitential rite.

If there is any portion of the liturgy where kneeling should be restored, it is the confession. Kneeling for prayer was universally practiced by the early Reformers. The only objection to kneeling emerging from that period was in connection with the reception of the sacrament. The objection was based on the fear that the elements might be worshiped if the people were to continue to kneel to receive the sacrament.

However, since liturgy incorporates different types of prayer, the practice of kneeling for all prayer is questionable. Standing is certainly appropriate to prayers of praise and thanksgiving. Kneeling might therefore be reserved for the prayers of confession and perhaps intercession. Clearly no bodily posture conveys penitence as effectively as the act of kneeling.

Although kneeling was the universal custom for centuries, it was finally largely replaced by standing for prayer. Standing for prayer also has strong precedent in ancient Israel. However, toward the end of the nineteenth century both standing and kneeling were generally abandoned in most Protestant traditions in preference to sitting for prayer. Of all the postures for prayer, sitting is the least suitable for corporate prayer, although it is appropriate for meditation. In this regard George F. Macleod, of Scotland's Iona Community, has observed:

> I have heard it often claimed the "Presbyterians" sit to pray. It is well to remember that for a long period they knelt and for a longer period they stood. It was less than a hundred years ago that Presbyterians first thought to be seated while in corporate prayer: having neither the church furniture that allowed of kneeling nor the old stamina that assisted them to stand.[60]

What is true of Presbyterian practice is true of most other Protestant traditions as well.

In an age when we tend to be too self-sufficient, a restoration of the practice of kneeling for at least the acts of penitence, and standing for all other prayers, might assist us to recognize our need for dependence upon God.

The case against kneeling is that it has less natural meaning to people than it once did. In our modern culture, kneeling is no longer customary apart from worship. People no longer bow or kneel before sovereigns of state. For this reason it may be inadvisable to try to introduce kneeling when it is not natural to the members of a particular congregation. Where kneeling seems unnatural, standing is surely the appropriate posture for all prayer. To remain seated for prayer has nothing in its favor, for its casualness fails to communicate a recognition of being in the presence of God. Because people are not able to concentrate for long periods while standing or kneeling, lengthy prayers need to be avoided. If kneeling is restored, it would of course require some provision for kneelers in the pews or chairs.

If confession is not an invariable part of the liturgy, it should be said at least during the penitential seasons of Advent and Lent, and at other times at the discretion of the minister. If Advent and Lent possess the penitential character inherent in them, it seems unnecessary to have a penitential rite at Christmas and Easter for which the prior seasons have prepared us. If the prayer of confession is omitted, the declaration of forgiveness might still be given, and a penitential petition could be made a part of the intercessions. Or, the declaration of pardon might be omitted on occasion when the Holy Communion is celebrated, regarding the sacrament itself as pardon.

5. THE LITURGY OF THE WORD

The Collect. The particular theme of the day may be briefly stated before praying the collect for the day. This short prayer which precedes the lessons offers in the form of a petition some meaning of the lessons that are to follow. Visual projections might occasionally be used with the collect to set the theme of a given celebration.

The Lessons. There is great value for a congregation to use the lessons provided in the lectionary. The lectionaries available to Lutherans, Episcopalians, Presbyterians, the United Church of Christ, the Disciples of Christ, and Methodists (as also the liturgical work of the Consultation on Church Union) are all based upon the Roman Catholic lectionary. Each tradition has made a few revisions appropriate for its own use, but the variations are few. The result is that a major segment of the church as a whole now has a common lectionary. Exegetical and expositional materials based on the lectionary abound.

The ecumenical values of using the lectionary are obvious. Using a lectionary enables the people to hear the full message of the Scripture over a period of time. They will not be restricted to the favorite passages of the preacher. It also provides an excellent discipline for the preacher, who will be called to the exposition of a wider selection of Scriptures and themes than perhaps he or she would otherwise provide. The lectionary offers an organized plan for acquainting the worshipers with the total content of Scripture. The Bible's wealth is so great, and the time available for reading it in public is so little, that careful planning is important. A consistent use of the lectionary is thus valuable to a full utilization of the riches of the Christian year.

The lessons should be read in the following order as a general practice: Old Testament, Epistle, and lastly Gospel. If any one of the lessons is omitted, the order still remains the same. Each reading may be introduced with brief comments that point out the specific relationship to the theme of the day or its ties with the other readings. This will help the worshipers understand the context and meaning of the lessons as they are read. The use of various translations may be profitable.

Lay persons trained in reading the Scripture may regularly read the lessons. Members of the congregation appointed to read the lessons may come from their places among the people to read, thereby making it a congregational action. Or, the lessons may be read from the midst of the assembly.

It is a very good practice for those reading the lessons to rehearse the readings several times prior to the service. In this way the flow of the action and the trend of the thoughts within the lesson may be discerned.

The lesson should be read without pomp, much in the manner of an able news reporter. The reader should use the same kind of emphasis, changes in tone, and variations in speed as one uses in conversation. A pause at the appropriate time will help convey the lesson's fullest meaning. Eyes should be kept on the page. During the reading of the Scripture there is no need to try to establish eye contact with the people. Care should be given to voice pitch, enunciation, and pronunciation. The reader ought to strive to make the lesson clearly understood. It is important that the reader read to be heard. If necessary, the voice should be properly amplified.

The lessons may from time to time lend themselves to other treatment than merely that of being read. They may be presented in simple dramatic form, such as several individuals reading the lines of the narrative. One reader may read the connecting portions, with other individuals or groups reading the lines spoken by the characters in the lesson. Some Scriptures might be done musically, or accompanied with live or recorded music. Others might be accompanied by visual projections, by colored light, or with dance. In all use of projections and dance, care must be taken to ensure that the visual element does not overpower the words of the lesson. The effects should enhance the meaning rather than detract from the readings. Ordinarily it is best to first read the lesson straight, then reread the lesson with the dance or other visual interpretation accompanying it.

Some congregations include a reading from modern authors in addition to the Scriptures. These may be selected in harmony with the theme established by the Scripture lessons, and may be chosen from a variety of sources, such as drama, literature, theological writings, and newspapers.

Psalms and Hymns. The singing of psalms, long a traditional part of the liturgy of the Word, might well be recovered in some form. The psalms are meant to be sung rather than read. It is appropriate to sing a psalm between the lessons. There are many styles of music to which psalms are set—both traditional and modern. A variety of styles can be incorporated. Psalms may be sung antiphonally, between a singer and the congregation or between the choir and the congregation. They are worthy of greater use among Protestants.

Proclamation. Both in location and in design, the pulpit should contribute to an intimacy between preacher and people. The pulpit is not just the place from which the Word is proclaimed. It also symbolizes the importance that the written and spoken Word has for the people of God. The pulpit should clearly convey the centrality of the Scripture. The Bible should therefore be the prominent feature of the pulpit, visible at all times. This might be achieved by providing a niche or front panel on the pulpit in which the Bible could be placed when not being read. Another possibility is a desk-like pulpit, with a wide surface. The preacher would read from the Bible at one end, then move to the other end for delivering the sermon.

The sermon should follow immediately upon the reading of the lessons to make clear the relationship between the Scripture and preaching. This is particularly important where the architectural arrangement includes a lectern from which the Bible is read. The use of both a lectern and a pulpit tends to divide lesson from sermon. Properly ordering the service will help overcome this division. Where a lectern is a part of the architectural furnishings, all that has been said above concerning the visibility of the Bible is equally appropriate for the design of the lectern.

The sermon does not always need to be preached from the pulpit. Preaching from a different location on certain occasions may contribute to more effective communication. The preacher may, for example, speak simply and informally in the aisle in the midst of the people, or at the holy table if the subject is the Lord's Supper, or at the font if the subject is Baptism.

For centuries preaching has been an important part of the Protestant liturgical tradition. However, it is questionable whether the average preacher can effectively engage a modern congregation in a sermon that lasts longer than twenty minutes.

Knowledge of communications is far ahead of its utilization within worship. There is great value in seeking a diversity of proclamation forms rather than having the proclamation invariably be in a monologue style. Other forms utilize all the senses and can effect a more total involvement of the worshipers.

The possibilities of different forms of proclamation are endless. They include the use of short films, followed by discussion. A sermon might be given a visual dimension through the use of slides or motion picture scenes, or through the use of an overhead projector during the sermon. Occasionally a photograph vividly interprets a Scripture lesson more effectively than any amount of verbal explanation. A panel of ministers and/or members of the congregation could discuss the Scripture for the day. It may take the form of a dialogue sermon in which someone is selected to pose questions or state reactions during the sermon (this should be carefully rehearsed). A specialist may be invited to speak, the congregation having the opportunity to ask questions afterward. Discussion may involve participation by the members of the congregation as a whole or in small groups. Brief dramatic presentations may be used, perhaps excerpts from plays. A taped recording with discussion is also a possibility.

Surely the exposition of Scripture need not be confined to the monologue of words of a preacher, and thus perpetuate the confusion between Word and words. Importance should not be attached to the inviolable nature of the sermon. But care should be taken that the Word is proclaimed in a manner that most effectively communicates the message.

However, since the visual is such a strong medium and can easily dominate, attention should be given to determine when, where, and how much visual material will enhance without taking over. The community, not a screen, is the focal point of worship. Overuse of projections can produce a passive congregation. Care should be taken to ensure that use of the visual involves people more deeply in the action of the liturgy.

If a church is going to be able to utilize most effectively other forms of proclamation than the sermon, a movable pulpit should be a distinct advantage. Portability of the pulpit would free the space it normally occupies so that it may be utilized for other forms of proclamation. Unencumbered space is a requirement for such forms as drama and dance.

Movable seating is also an advantage to provide more easily for discussion, especially when the congregation breaks up into small discussion groups within the context of the liturgy.

The Creed. It seems unnecessary to recite one of the traditional creeds every Sunday, but there is value in their frequent use to enable people to identify more readily with Christians of previous centuries. Creeds therefore belong in the liturgy, especially at major festivals. Traditionally the Nicene Creed is used at all festivals and whenever the Lord's Supper is celebrated. Since the Apostles' Creed began as a baptismal formula, it is appropriate to use it at baptisms.

Opportunity should be given a congregation occasionally to sing the creed, especially on festival occasions. Singing the creed enables people to see it more readily as poetic imagery rather than only as a literal expression of personal belief.

Modern creedal statements may also be used, such as the one of the United Church of Christ. United Presbyterians might use portions of The Confession of 1967, even though it was not written for liturgical usage. A creedal type of hymn could occasionally replace the creed, such as the Te Deum, "O God, You Are the Father," "Sing Praise to God, Who Reigns Above," "God Has Spoken—by His Prophets," or "We Believe in One True God."

When saying the creed, the ministers and those assisting in worship should face the holy table along with the congregation, thus identifying themselves as a part of the believing people of God.

Baptism. Baptism is most appropriately placed in relationship to the creed after the sermon, as response to the Word read and proclaimed.

A major emphasis of the Reformed tradition has been the communal nature of Baptism, since it is the sacrament of incorporation into the body of Christ. The entire fellowship of God's people participate in it. Therefore private Baptism has been discouraged.

As stated above, consideration might be given to restoring the place of Baptism to a position just inside the worship room at the main entrance into the nave. Calvin called for the placing of the font in front of the people primarily for audio reasons and in the belief that such a position stresses the communal nature of the sacrament. In pre-Reformation church buildings, fonts were located in rooms separated from the nave. Baptism was privately administered. By having the font close to the pulpit, the relationship of Baptism to the Word was thought to be more apparent. None of these concerns needs to be sacrificed in placing the font at the main entrance into the nave. In such a position, the congregation's participation is not sacrificed and entry into the body of Christ through Baptism is more forcefully symbolized. In such a conspicuous position, the font reminds each Christian of his or her own Baptism each time he or she enters or leaves the building. If the place of Baptism is thus removed from the pulpit and table area, each liturgical center will have its own appropriate space and be able to maintain its own distinct integrity. The relationship of Baptism to the Eucharist and the Word is more clearly seen, Baptism being the entry into that fellowship where Word and Eucharist mark the continuing style of the Christian's liturgical life.

There is also something to be said in favor of a baptistry in which one must step down into the font area. Stepping down symbolizes identification with Christ's death and burial. Stepping up after Baptism symbolizes rising with Christ to newness of life.

Ample space surrounding the font adds to the importance of the sacrament. Significance will also be given to the sacrament if the font is of sufficient prominence and size. However, the font should speak clearly that it is a receptacle for water. Water is the most important thing in Baptism and water should be the prominent thing about the font. This is easier to recognize if the font contains a large amount of water.

The relationship of Baptism to the ministry of the Holy Spirit may be expressed in some artistic manner in the space provided for the sacrament.

In the act of Baptism, drama is added when there is a procession to the font on the part of minister, lay assistant, parents, family, and friends who then stand about the font. The first portion of the baptismal rite—the baptismal questions and the creed—might take place near the holy table. The procession would then move to the font, if it is located at the entrance, where the Baptism itself would take place. An appropriate psalm (such as Psalm 42) or hymn may be sung as a part of the procession. The remainder of the congregation may easily participate in the rite while standing at their seats facing in the direction of the font. If water is not in the font at all times, water may be poured into the font before the service, or it may be poured into the font as a part of the rite before the prayer which immediately precedes the Baptism. In this way, the sound and sight of water gives added emphasis that water is the principal element of the sacrament. In the Baptism itself, the minister should use an ample amount of water rather than simply place a moistened hand upon the candidate's forehead. The minister should fill the palm of his or her hand with water (or better, use a baptismal shell) and pour the water over the head of the recipient, once . . . twice . . . three times. Baptismal towels should be nearby.

Such attention given to the practice of Baptism will help to restore its significance and give it the place it deserves in the liturgical life of the church.

The Commissioning of Baptized Persons (Confirmation). The commissioning of baptized persons is also appropriately placed in relationship to the creed after the sermon, as response to the Word read and proclaimed.

In the New Testament, hands were laid upon the apostles as they were commissioned to go out to engage in mission. The laying on of hands is an appropriate practice for the commissioning of youth to their Christian service in the world. Each candidate would kneel and the pastor would place his or her hands upon each one in the act of commissioning.

Concerns of the Church. Announcements concerning the life of the parish may be given immediately preceding the prayers of the people. Such placement makes them a part of the prayer concern of the congregation. If an announcement would not be an appropriate subject for prayer, it may be that it is not appropriate within the context of worship. Community matters as well as parish activities and concerns might be included. If announcements appear in the bulletin, they need not be repeated orally.

The congregation may be encouraged to submit written concerns for prayer before the service, which would then be included in the prayers. Before the prayers, the minister and/or members may mention the specific petitions, intercessions, and thanksgiving that were submitted. Or, the pastor might move down into the midst of the people, and invite the people to share their concerns verbally. The minister may also mention the death of a member of the congregation.

Prayers of the People. It is particularly meaningful that when the pastor leads the people in the prayers while standing in their midst or near them, he or she turn to face in the same direction as the people. More than any other position, this readily conveys the understanding that the prayers are the prayers of the people. Prayers offered at the pulpit too easily imply a praying to the people, and give the impression that the pastor is praying alone rather than representing the people in prayer.

If the prayers are not offered from a position near or in the midst of the people, the table is the best place from which to lead the people in prayer, the pastor standing behind the table.

A bidding prayer is an effective way to help people involve themselves in the prayer. In a bidding prayer, following an opening petition, the people are invited to pray about a particular concern. There is a period of unhurried silence. The minister then concludes that concern with a brief petition, the people responding with "Amen" or "Hear our prayer, O God." The people are then invited to pray about another concern. Silence again follows, the minister prays, and the people respond. The cycle is repeated for as many concerns as are appropriate to the situation. After the last concern, the minister concludes with a final petition summing up the period of intercession. As a variation, the bidding prayer might be divided among members of the congregation, who give the bidding and the prayer from their particular place amid the people. When lay persons offer the petitions, the pastor could offer the opening petition and conclude the prayers with the final petition, or these could be unison prayers. The response of "Amen" or "Hear our prayer, O God" should be encouraged, since this makes the prayer the prayer of all, rather than only of the one who voices it.

The biddings may effectively be in the form of reading lead sentences from news articles of the week. This is helpful to assist people to recognize that the prayers of the people are in fact to be rooted in the life of the world. Some or all of the petitions may be prepared locally so that they might be as current and fresh as the morning newspaper. They should be specific, using names when possible, and refer to concrete situations instead of being generalizations only.

Another effective means of intercession is a litany. The litany form may also incorporate extemporary prayer for specific current concerns.

Prayers from contemporary collections may also be used, such as those of Malcolm Boyd, Michel Quoist, or Caryl Micklem.

Still another variation in intercession is to invite the people themselves to offer prayers in the form of sentences each embodying a petition.

The use of such varying forms as have been suggested will result in a desirable flexibility and variety in the prayers of the people. In all intercessory prayer forms, care should be taken to seek to develop a concern that includes not only the immediate concerns of the congregation but the concerns of the world at large as well. The world and community should be fully represented in the concerns and the prayers of the people.

If the congregation has provisions to kneel for prayer, the people should be invited to kneel for the intercessions as well as the confession. If the congregation has no such provision, let them stand.

The Peace. The peace may be initiated by the minister and then taken up by everyone in the congregation in an almost spontaneous manner resulting in a moment of joyous informality and community intimacy. Let the people greet those beside, in front of, and behind them. The minister(s) might also move among the people to greet them. This may be done with ease if the minister has stood with the people in the prayers. The ushers might be instructed to note the persons in the congregation who are visitors or who are not well known, and go to them extending them the peace.

Taking the other person's hand in both of yours, or giving a handshake, or using some other appropriate gesture are possible ways. Use of the first name of the person makes the greeting warm and personal.

The peace may be appropriately exchanged at other places in the liturgy rather than after the intercessions. It might be made a part of the call to worship, or follow the declaration of pardon, or precede the prayers of the people. It might be appropriate before or after the invitation to the Lord's Supper is given, or just before the distribution of the Communion elements. It might also be exchanged at the end of the liturgy, following the dismissal.

In a service using visuals, an appropriate picture could be projected on the wall as background to the exchange.

6. THE LITURGY OF THANKS

Offering. Historically, the offertory has referred principally to the presentation of the elements of bread and wine for the sacrament. But the term has also come to refer to the tithes and gifts of money that support the church. The offertory appropriately combines the presentation of wine and bread with the presentation of the money.

There is no need for ushers to come forward to receive the offering plates. They may be carried from the narthex.

Self-conscious precision or military mannerisms should be avoided, because they introduce a formalism that is unnecessary and detracts from the natural spirit of worship.

All should participate in the offering. The ministers and choir as well as the congregation should be presented with the opportunity to give in the context of worship. Concrete examples as to what the money is used for may be stated at the time of the announcements. It should be clear that the community is concerned with a broader ministry than merely maintaining its own existence.

Instead of (or in addition to) an offertory hymn, anthem, or organ selection, audio-visuals may be used. The growth and harvest in nature, or of human giving and receiving, may be depicted. Projections might also develop the offering of self to service to God and the world. Mission is surely a part of offertory, and may be developed visually. When we see the offertory as relating to commitment, other possibilities unfold.

The act of collecting the money should be done quickly and simply. Emphasis should be upon the presentation rather than the collection. The wine and the bread should be brought at this time as a part of the offering, along with the gifts of money—first, the gifts of money, then the bread and the wine.

Some congregations have introduced the bringing of food staples for distribution to the poor in instances of need on a particular Sunday of the month. These also should be brought forward at the presentation.

The money should always be presented at the holy table after it has been received, for it is an important part of the liturgy. In the offertory presentation, the congregation is unified. The offering should then be placed on a table or a ledge provided for that purpose near the table. For the sake of an uncrowded table it is preferable that the money gifts not be placed on the table itself. Furthermore, the money gifts do not relate directly to the Lord's Supper. Certainly the offering should not be whisked away to be counted during the latter part of the service, but be left in its place until after the dismissal.

A meaningful variation would be introduced for representatives from the congregation, other than the ushers, to participate in the presentation, whether or not they shared in the collection itself. Here is an opportunity for the children to participate as gift bearers. A family, including several generations when possible, might be gift bearers on a given Sunday.

On occasion the congregation may form a procession and bring their own offerings to the holy table, where they are received.

Families in the congregation might sign up to take turns to provide the bread and wine for the Eucharist. A family may wish to make the bread in their own kitchen. Providing home-baked bread makes it clear that the bread and wine are something we give out of our lives. The family providing the bread and wine will accompany the ushers to the table. If the bread is home-baked, it should be brought preferably by the person who baked it. The bread should be a whole loaf and unbroken.

It is most meaningful when the bread is a loaf, rather than the familiar diced bread (which is unlike any other method of serving or using bread) or wafers (which are unlike any form of bread in common use). The use of a single common loaf is more symbolically appropriate, for it signifies that in partaking of the one loaf Jesus Christ, we together become one body (I Cor. 10:17). It speaks of the essential unity of the body of Christ. Both cubed bread and wafers reinforce the individuality some people bring to the sacrament. The bread ought to be tasty and attractive, and have substance to it. It should have a soft crust, be easy to break, and not prone to crumble.

Wine is preferable to grape juice, in example of the upper room, and for the symbolism involved. Wine, in contrast to grape juice, is expressive of joy and delight. Grape juice can never become a symbol of exhilaration. The Lord's Supper is a special occasion—a banquet and feast—therefore, the wine should be of good quality. If a common cup is used in the distribution, the bottle might be brought forward, which is later poured in the presence of the people into a flagon. In those congregations where wine is not readily accepted by everyone, personal convictions can be respected by providing both wine and grape juice in the distribution. This is a simple matter when serving from a chalice, for two chalices can be used—one for the wine, the other for grape juice. The people may be clearly instructed in the order of service folder as to which is wine and which is grape juice. Furthermore, when serving the people at the table, wine can be served from one end of the table and grape juice from the other. Some churches now provide white wine in the Communion glasses of the outer circle of the tray, with red grape juice in the rest of the glasses. Little instruction is necessary in this instance, for the color identifies the choice. It might be noted that white wine is often used in those churches which traditionally use wine for the sacrament.

The offertory hymn or *a* doxology (which should vary from the almost universal use of Thomas Ken's "Doxology") should be sung lustily as the procession leaves the narthex to approach the table with the gifts. There is no need for the pastor to offer a prayer in addition to the sung offertory hymn; he or she should move quickly to the introductory words of the Lord's Supper, or to the versicles leading into the prayer of thanksgiving.

Weekly Communion. The norm of Christian worship has for centuries been a service of both Word *and* sacrament. In the pre-Reformation Church, the preached Word had been largely lost. The Reformation sought to restore the preached

Word to its earlier prominence and glory. But the Reformers had no intention of losing the prominence of the sacrament. For example, John Calvin throughout his lifetime not only sought to give preaching a prominent place in worship but also desired that the people communicate weekly. He never achieved the pattern of weekly Communion, because of Zwinglian influence among the people and stubborn Genevan magistrates. However, while he was pastor of the church in Strasbourg, the sacrament was celebrated weekly in the cathedral and once each month in the parish churches. The practice of celebrating four times a year—Christmas, Easter, Pentecost, and the first Sunday of September—became the rule in Geneva. In 1561 Calvin left a record of his disappointment with the Genevan practice: "I have taken care to record publically that our custom is defective, so that those who come after me may be able to correct it the more freely and easily."[61]

But for four centuries, Protestant worship has been primarily a preaching service rather than a service of Word *and* sacrament. There are now evidences that this is being corrected. Gradually the sacrament is being celebrated more frequently in an increasing number of congregations.

Perhaps one reason why there is a move to more frequent Communion is that it involves all the senses. In the sacrament, taste, touch, and smell as well as sight and sound are involved. The sacrament gets beyond the merely verbal and communicates the gospel through all the senses. It is interesting to note that infrequency of celebration has seemed to characterize forms of worship that are predominantly verbal.

It is a worthy objective to move steadily toward a celebration of the sacrament as the main service of each Lord's Day, rather than placing it mechanically into a calendar, calling for its observance quarterly or on the first Sunday of each month. The desire of the people should determine how frequently they communicate. Instead, we limit the desire of some by allowing them opportunity only on a quarterly or monthly basis.

Objections are often made that weekly celebration would make the sacrament commonplace. But weekly prayer does not make prayer commonplace. Weekly preaching does not make the sermon commonplace. If we were to restore a weekly celebration of the sacrament, we might find that instead of making the Eucharist commonplace and ordinary, it might come to have greater meaning in the life of the communicant and in the fellowship of the community of faith.

Another objection to weekly Communion is that it would result in unduly lengthening all services, since the Communion service is often longer than other services. This need not be the case if attention is given to methods of serving that do not prolong the action. The wine may be served immediately following the bread rather than each comprising a separate serving. This will cut the serving time in half. The use of more persons in serving the elements will also conserve time. This can be done without a loss of dignity or a feeling of time pressure. The service will not be unduly lengthened if care is taken to limit the length of sermon, prayers, readings, and hymns and to avoid needless announcements. Such will be beneficial, for it will quicken the pace of the service.

The Eucharistic Prayer. Since the eucharistic prayer is liturgy's greatest act of praise, it is proper for the congregation to stand during the prayer.

Before the minister begins the prayer, celebrant and people engage in a dialogue. The people are invited to join together in praising and thanking God for his greatness. The dialogue begins: "Lift up your hearts." In response, the people affirm that they do join together in lifting their hearts "to the Lord." The classic dialogue continues: "Let us give thanks to the Lord our God." "It is right to give him thanks and praise." The versicle should be exchanged joyfully, briskly and cordially, the hands of the celebrant free of books or papers. Voice and hands should express the festive intent of the words.

The prayer should be positive and joyful, never sullen, sober, slow, or sad. It is not a morbid moment. The fact that God lives should move us to eucharistic excitement.

This is an instance in which there is great value in projecting on the wall the portions to be said by the congregation. The people's faces would be lifted up away from service book or bulletin, which is appropriate to this prayer, a prayer that is actually midway between hymn and prayer.

Other eucharistic prayers may be borrowed or written. With increased frequency of celebration, a variation in the liturgical text will seem necessary in most congregations. If the pastor writes the eucharistic prayer, the basic elements of the prayer should be kept in mind—the thanksgiving and praise for God's love in creation and throughout history. It should also include a memorial of the life, death, and resurrection of Jesus Christ. It should emphasize the meaning of the Spirit of God present with his people, and climax in some sort of closing thanksgiving. The prayer might relate in some way to the theme of the particular worship of the day. Use of the prefaces provided for the church year adds specific seasonal meanings and variety. Thanks may be quite specific, relating to particular questions of life.

The Sanctus ("Holy, holy, holy . . .") should be sung with gusto, especially for the lines, "Blessed is he who comes in the name of the Lord. Hosanna in the highest."

The Breaking of Bread. The words of institution (I Cor. 11:23–26) may accompany the breaking of the bread and the pouring of the wine into the chalice. The movement at this point is suggestive and communicates effectively.

At the words "took bread," let the celebrant take the loaf of bread into both hands. At the words "broke it," the action of the Last Supper is repeated by the breaking of the loaf. The celebrant holds up toward the congregation the two fragments of the loaf while saying, "This is my body, which is for you . . ." The bread is then replaced on the tray while the words "Do this, remembering me" are said. (After the words of institution, the bread is further broken up as will be needed.)

The wine is then poured into a chalice from a flagon. Lifting the chalice with both hands, the celebrant says, "In the same way, he took the cup after supper . . ." The chalice is replaced on the table while the words "Do this, remembering me" are said. With hands outstretched over or toward the bread and wine the celebrant concludes with the words: "Every time you eat this bread and drink the cup. . . ."

If the parallel words are lifted from the Gospels for this portion, instead of the words of Paul, let similar acts be done.

Communion. There is great value in the people receiving the sacrament at the table rather than merely in its presence. It is more personal and intimate.

The custom under John Calvin was for the people to gather about the table on three sides where they received the sacrament from the hands of the minister. The minister officiated from behind the table in the basilican posture. Elsewhere in Europe (especially in Scotland and Holland), Reformed congregations celebrated seated about tables in meal fashion.

In receiving the sacrament at the table one more readily senses his or her place within the family of God than when the sacrament is received in the pew.

Pew Communion can be traced to Zwingli in Zurich, where a low view of the sacrament prevailed. The practice was adopted by English Independents, but for nearly three hundred years it was stoutly resisted by the Scots. But in the early part of the nineteenth century the practice began to be adopted among some city churches of Scotland, in spite of condemnations of the practice by Scottish General Assemblies. Gradually the practice became quite general. In the

United States, the custom is the result of Puritan and pietist influence. Pew Communion tends to be quite individualistic in nature.

For all to sit at the table, in the classic Reformed manner, may pose numerous problems if Communion is frequent. The preferred method of serving in regular practice is therefore surely to have the people stand about the table to receive the sacrament.

There is value in using a common chalice as well as a common loaf in serving the people. Thus the unity of the people in Christ is given expression. For those who consider this practice to be unsanitary, the method of intinction may be encouraged, in which the piece of bread is dipped into the wine and then eaten. If both wine and grape juice are served, a chalice will need to be provided for each.

If the congregation continues the practice of pew Communion instead of coming to the table or sitting at table, several chalices might be used. These could be filled from the flagon following the breaking of the bread into the number of fragments for distribution.

Where the serving is about the table, the ushering should be kept at a minimum, if it is needed at all, the people forming their own procession. Regimentation should be avoided.

There is much to be said in preference to a continuous Communion instead of serving "by tables." There is less awkwardness, such as signals to approach, words of dismissal, and signals to depart. It is also less time-consuming. The continuous Communion more readily unites the entire congregation together in the sacrament rather than just those at each individual "table."

The spirit during the serving should do nothing to jeopardize the triumphal nature of the feast. Penitential hymns should be avoided, except perhaps during penitential seasons. The time should not drag wearily but have a briskness about it.

In the folk type of celebration, consideration might be given to the use of a ceramic vessel for the wine rather than a silver chalice.

To encourage a greater quantity of bread being eaten and wine drunk helps to convey something of the feast or banquet sense of the sacrament.

There may be silence during Communion, or it may be interspersed with hymns, anthems, organ music, other instrumental music, or a restrained use of projections or dance.

Post-Communion. The post-Communion response should be sung or said buoyantly and forcefully, with vigor and excitement.

The closing should be in the spirit of triumphant praise, and move quickly and decisively without needless ceremonial or delay.

The dismissal is the final action of the liturgical gathering, in which the people are charged to go out to serve God. The people whom God has called together in worship are now sent out to speak and act for him. God assigns the task to make real in the world what is known and experienced in the gathering about the Lord's Table. Liturgy as "the work of the people," which begins in the gathering of the community of faith, now moves outward into the structures of society, where the people of God become an instrument of God to reconcile and heal life's brokenness.

The benediction is not the end; it is a beginning. In the benediction, the people are dismissed to go forth to engage in the work to which God has commissioned them.

Postscript

Far from being an escape from life's complexities and dilemmas, worship recenters us upon the hope of life and its possibilities. Worship engages us in the task of healing human brokenness, involves us in the work of building up everything that leads to human fulfillment.

Liturgy about the table and liturgy in the world are thus two faces of a single reality—the Christian life-style. Each is dependent upon the other. If worship fails to lead the community of faith into an engagement in God's work, worship will become self-serving, esoteric, and merely aesthetic. Apart from a unity with mission, worship tends to be sterile and out of touch with life. On the other hand, if service in the world is not rooted in worship, it will be aimless. Unless the liturgy of praise of God is united with the liturgy of work in God's world, both are impoverished. The union of both worship and service gives depth and direction to both. Each is vital to the other.

Worship needs to give meaning and direction to life, in relating us to God, who is the life-giving presence in the depths of life. If worship fails to do this, it fails to convey that which best contributes to human growth and wholeness. Therefore, for a human future, liturgical renewal is of crucial importance. Life needs depth. We can ill afford to have the word of hope pushed to the edge of life. Liturgical renewal can help prevent this from happening.

The community of faith at worship is the pinnacle of the church's life together. The congregation that knows a revitalization of its worship will discover the fountain from which flow life and hope into the world.

May God give us a new sense of the importance of the community of faith bound together in God's love. May God guide us in every attempt to renew the life-giving center of that community—the liturgy.

Notes

1. Edward Schillebeeckx, *God, the Future of Man,* tr. by N. D. Smith (Sheed & Ward, Inc., 1968), p. 84.

2. David Willis, "Piety: Sound and Substance," *Pacific Theological Review,* Vol. VI, No. 2 (1974), p. 16.

3. Margaret Mead, *Twentieth Century Faith: Hope and Survival* (Harper & Row, Publishers, Inc., 1972), p. 127.

4. *Ibid.,* p. 159.

5. Raimundo Panikkar, "Secularization and Worship," in *Worship and Secularization,* ed. by Wiebe Vos (Bussum, Holland: Paul Brand), p. 69.

6. *Ibid.*

7. John A. T. Robinson, *The Human Face of God* (The Westminster Press, 1973), p. 236.

8. "Constitution on the Sacred Liturgy," *The Documents of Vatican II,* ed. by Walter M. Abbott and Joseph Gallagher (Guild Press, America Press, and Association Press, 1966), Ch. i, Art. 7.

9. James F. White, *New Forms of Worship* (Abingdon Press, 1971), p. 149.

10. "The Directory for the Worship of God," *The Constitution of The United Presbyterian Church in the United States of America, Part II, Book of Order* (Philadelphia: The Office of the General Assembly of The United Presbyterian Church in the United States of America, 1967), Ch. III, Sec. 1.

11. *Ibid.,* Ch. III, Sec. 3.

12. *Ibid.*

13. *Ibid.,* Ch. VI, Sec. 1.

14. John A. T. Robinson, *Liturgy Coming to Life* (London: A. R. Mowbray & Co., Ltd., 1960), p. 22.

15. Scott Francis Brenner, *Ways of Worship for New Forms of Mission* (Friendship Press, 1968), p. 66.

16. Arthur A. Vogel, *Is the Last Supper Finished? Secular Light on a Sacred Meal* (Sheed & Ward, Inc., 1968), p. 151.

17. Norman Perrin, *Rediscovering the Teaching of Jesus* (London: SCM Press, Ltd., 1967), pp. 102–105.

18. Charles Davis, *Liturgy and Doctrine: The Doctrinal Basis of the Liturgical Movement* (London: Sheed & Ward, Ltd., 1960), p. 10.

19. James F. White, *The Worldliness of Worship* (Oxford University Press, 1967), p. 172.

20. Arnold Come, "Christians in Both Church and World," *Laity,* Vol. XVI (November 1963), p. 26.

21. Marianne H. Micks, *The Future Present: The Phenomenon of Christian Worship* (The Seabury Press, Inc., 1970), p. 178.

22. Norman Pittenger, *Life as Eucharist* (Wm. B. Eerdmans Publishing Company, 1973), p. 99.

23. The Commission on Worship of the Consultation on Church Union, *An Order of Worship* (Forward Movement Publications, 1968), p. 30.

24. J. G. Davies, *Worship and Mission* (London: SCM Press, Ltd., 1966), p. 36.

25. Pittenger, *Life as Eucharist,* p. 78.

26. Robinson, *Liturgy Coming to Life,* p. 16.

27. J. J. von Allmen, *Worship: Its Theology and Practice,* tr. by Harold Knight and W. Fletcher Fleet (London: Lutterworth Press, 1965), pp. 55, 56.

28. *The Worshipbook—Services and Hymns* (The Westminster Press, 1972), p. 38. Changes are incorporated that are suggested in David G. Buttrick, "Proposed Corrections to Liturgical Portions of the Worshipbook," *Reformed Liturgy and Music,* Vol. VIII (Fall 1974), p. 27.

29. Edward A. Sovik, "Liturgical Art and the New Churches," *Response,* Vol. I (Advent 1959), p. 14.

30. Howard Moody, "Worship as Celebration and Confrontation," in *Multi-Media Worship: A Model and Nine Viewpoints,* ed. by Myron B. Bloy, Jr. (The Seabury Press, Inc., 1969), p. 89.

31. Howard Moody, "Revolution in Liturgy: An Interim Report on a Work of Worship in Progress," *Andover Newton Quarterly,* Vol. II (January 1971), p. 117.

32. *Ibid.*

33. Luther D. Reed, *Worship: A Study of Corporate Devotion* (Muhlenberg Press, 1959), p. 382.

34. Trevor Wyatt Moore, "A Rationale for Christian Art," *Journal of the American Society for Church Architects,* No. 8 (February 1967), pp. 48, 49.

35. *Ibid.,* p. 49.

36. Daniel Berrigan, "The Catholic Dream World and the Sacred Image," *Worship,* Vol. XXX (1960–1961), p. 559.

37. Gerardus van der Leeuw, *Sacred and Profane Beauty: The Holy in Art,* tr. by David E. Green (Holt, Rinehart & Winston, Inc., 1963), p. 13.

38. *Ibid.,* p. 36.

39. *Ibid.,* p. 35.

40. Doug Adams, *Congregational Dancing in Christian Worship* (Doug Adams, 1971), available from The Enabling Company, 1035 Indiana Street, Vallejo, Calif. 94590; Lucien Deiss and Gloria Weyman, *Dancing for God* (World Library Publication, Inc., 1969); Margaret Fisk Taylor, *A Time to Dance: Symbolic Movement in Worship* (United Church Press, 1967); Marilee Zdenek and Marge Champion, *Catch the New Wind* (Word Books, 1972); Carla De Sola, *The Spirit Moves: A Handbook of Dance and Prayer* (Washington, D.C.: The Liturgical Conference, 1977), available from The Liturgical Conference, 1221 Massachusetts Avenue, N.W., Washington D.C. 20005. A helpful multimedia kit *Liturgical Dance* in the series *Worship and the Arts* is available from The Joint Office of Worship, 1044 Alta Vista Road, Louisville, Ky. 40205.

41. Van der Leeuw, *Sacred and Profane Beauty,* p. 43.

42. Daniel A. Kister, "Dance and Theater in Christian Worship," *Worship,* Vol. XL (December 1971), p. 594.

43. *Ibid.,* p. 595.

44. *Ibid.,* pp. 595, 596.

45. *Ibid.,* p. 596.

46. *Plays for the Church* (New York: Department of Church and Culture, Division of Christian Life and Mission, National Council of Churches, 1966). Guidance is available from The Ecumenical Council for Drama and Other Arts, Inc., 9103 Queenston Drive, St. Louis, Mo. 63126, Wilma Ringstrom, founder. A helpful multimedia kit *Drama* is available in the series *Worship and the Arts* (see address in note 40).

47. Editorial, *Albuquerque Journal,* Nov. 26, 1974, p. 4.

48. Church bulletin, St. Andrew United Presbyterian Church, Albuquerque, New Mexico, Dec. 7, 1974.

49. Erich Fromm, *The Revolution of Hope: Toward a Humanized Technology* (Bantam Books, Inc., 1968), p. 9.

50. *Ibid.,* p. 13.

51. Heinz Werner Zimmermann, "Church Music in a Pluralistic Society," *Music Ministry,* Vol. IV (March 1972), p. 10.

52. *Ibid.*

53. Erik Routley, *Words, Music and the Church* (Abingdon Press, 1968), p. 207.

54. *Ibid.*

55. Dennis Fitzpatrick, "A View from the Far Left," in *Crisis in Church Music?* (Washington, D.C.: The Liturgical Conference, 1967), pp. 84–85.

56. C. Alexander Peloquin, "In Praise of Joy—The Left Position," in *Crisis in Church Music?* pp. 75–76.

57. Collections of Gelineau Psalms, training tapes and recordings, as well as other responsorial psalms, are available from G.I.A. Publications, Inc., 7404 S. Mason Avenue, Chicago, Ill. 60638. Ideas for the creative use of music in worship are available in the multimedia kits *Sounding Praise* and *Sharing the Spirit in Music* in the series *Worship and the Arts* (see address in note 40).

58. John Killinger, *Leave It to the Spirit: Commitment and Freedom in the New Liturgy* (Harper & Row, Publishers, Inc., 1971), pp. 185–186.

59. Marion P. Ireland, *Textile Art in the Church: Vestments, Paraments, and Hangings in Contemporary Worship, Art, and Architecture* (Abingdon Press, 1971), p. 25.

60. George F. Macleod, *Only One Way Left: Church Prospect,* 3d ed. (Glasgow: The Iona Community, 1961), p. 100.

61. Karl Gottlieb Bretschneider, *Corpus Reformatorum,* Vol. XXXVIII, i, p. 213.